Essential
Istanbul

by Sylvie Franquet & Anthony Sattin

Sylvie Franquet studied Arabic at the universities of Ghent, Tunis and Cairo, where she lived for six years, working as a model, translator and tour manager. She writes for the Belgian newspaper *De Morgen*. Anthony Sattin, a regular contributor on travel and literature to the *Sunday Times*, is the author of *Shooting the Breeze*, a novel, and *Lifting the Veil*, a history of travellers and tourists in Egypt from 1768 to 1956. He also discovered Florence Nightingale's *Letters from Egypt*. Together they have written several books for the AA (on Egypt, Tunisia, the Greek Islands, Bangkok, Brussels & Bruges, and Morocco).

Byzantine fresco in a dome of the Kariye Camii

AA Publishing

Written by Sylvie Franquet & Anthony Sattin

Produced by AA Publishing.
© The Automobile Association 1999
Maps © The Automobile Association 1999

Distributed in the United Kingdom by AA Publishing,
Norfolk House, Priestley Road, Basingstoke, Hampshire,
RG24 9NY.

A CIP catalogue record for this book is available from the
British Library.

ISBN 0 7495 1914 2

The contents of this publication are believed correct at
the time of printing. Nevertheless, the publishers cannot
be held responsible for any errors or omissions or for
changes in the details given in this guide or for the
consequences of any reliance on the information provided
by the same. Assessments of attractions, hotels,
restaurants and so forth are based upon the authors' own
experience and, therefore, descriptions given in this guide
necessarily contain an element of subjective opinion which
may not reflect the publisher's opinion or dictate a reader's
own experience on another occasion.

We have tried to ensure accuracy in this guide, but
things do change and we would be grateful if readers
would advise us of any inaccuracies they may encounter.

Published by AA Publishing, a trading name of Automobile
Association Developments Limited, whose registered
office is Norfolk House, Priestley Road, Basingstoke,
Hampshire, RG24 9NY.
Registered number 1878835.

Colour separation: Pace Colour, Southampton
Printed and bound in Italy by Printer Trento srl

Above: *traditional Turkish attire*

Front cover: *a view over the domes and minarets of Sultanahmet Camii; Turkey is famous for its carpets; street vendor selling grape juice*
Back cover: *multi-coloured spices on sale in the Spice Bazaar*

Find out more about
AA Publishing and the
wide range of services
the AA provides by
visiting our web site at
www.theaa.co.uk

Contents

About this Book

Essential *Istanbul* is divided into five sections to cover the most important aspects of your visit to Istanbul.

Viewing Istanbul pages 5–14
An introduction to Istanbul by the authors
Istanbul's Features
Essence of Istanbul
The Shaping of Istanbul
Peace and Quiet
Istanbul's Famous

Top Ten pages 15–26
The authors' choice of the Top Ten places to see in Istanbul, in alphabetical order, each with practical information.

What to See pages 27–90
Two sections: Istanbul and Istanbul Excursions, each with its own brief introduction and an alphabetical listing of the main attractions
Practical information
Snippets of 'Did You Know…' information
7 suggested walks/tours
2 features

Where To... pages 91–116
Detailed listings of the best places to eat, stay, shop, take the children and be entertained.

Practical Matters pages 117–24
A highly visual section containing essential travel information.

Maps
All map references are to the individual maps found in the What to See section of this guide.
For example, the Sultanahmet Camii has the reference ➕ 39E2 – indicating the page on which the map is located and the grid square in which the mosque is to be found.
A list of the maps that have been used in this travel guide can be found in the index.

Prices
Where appropriate, an indication of the cost of an establishment is given by £ signs:
£££ denotes higher prices, **££** denotes average prices, while **£** denotes lower prices.

Star Ratings
Most of the places described in this book have been given a rating:
✪✪✪ Do not miss
✪✪ Highly recommended
✪ Worth seeing

Viewing
Istanbul

Above: *the massive central dome
of Aya Sofya*
Right: *a colourful folk music player*

5

Our Istanbul

Istanbulis

Take time, even if you have little of it, to meet Istanbulis and watch them go about their business, for they are traders at heart and the whole city is a market. They are, in general, very friendly people, accustomed to dealing with foreigners, and their hospitality is famous. They have a strong sense of hierarchy and respect, something inherited from their Ottoman ancestors, and when it comes to greetings you will find they can be polite to the point of excess.

Istanbul sits astride two continents – Europe and Asia – and has two distinct characters. It is a city where you can get lost in dazzling bazaars and find a welcome in sophisticated Western restaurants, where you can be thrilled by the sight of antiquity (a fountain here, a column there) and surprised by glimpses of modernity (mobile phones and international fashion designers), where you can be overwhelmed by Imperial Byzantine and Ottoman architecture, yet staggered by a pace of development so rapid that map-makers cannot keep up.

Originally built, like Rome, across seven hills, Istanbul is now so large it feels more like a series of cities, each with its own distinct and fascinating character. Again like Rome, the scale of the place might suggest that it is not an obvious city for walking. Yet within each particular area – and especially in the historic centre – we find it easiest to get around on foot. That way there is always the chance of surprise meetings and extraordinary sights, of mosques and monuments that delight the spirit, and tea houses, sweet-shops and bars that please the appetite.

For all the splendid legacies of a proud past, Istanbul has its critics, who complain about lack of green spaces, traffic jams and pollution. Yet escape is simple: jump on a boat and cruise the Bosphorus or take a trip across the Sea of Marmara to the Princes' Islands. What's more, you can look forward to your return at the end of the day, for this city of romance looks its best from the water and there is no more evocative way to reach it than by boat.

Fishing from Galata Bridge is an institution

Istanbul's Features

Population

During the reign of Süleyman the Magnificent (1520–1566), when Paris had 250,000 inhabitants, Constantinople (as Istanbul was then called) was the biggest city in the world, with a population of 700,000. In 1960 the population was 1.8 million. The current population is something of a mystery. Depending on who you ask, it can be anything from 10 to 15 million, though officially it is around 12 million. A 1995 *New York Times* article reported that on average some 500,000 people a year move into the city. Istanbulis joke that there are about as many trying to get out. A fifth of Turkey's population now lives in Istanbul. Like Rome, on which it was modelled by Emperor Constantine, the city was originally built on seven hills. Now Istanbul (properly İstanbul) has only 2sq m of green space per person, less than any other city in Europe, but it is working hard to re-create more green spaces, particularly along the waterfronts.

Climate

Spring is the best time to visit, when the parks and the Bosphorus are green and breezes from the Black Sea blow away the winter smog. Autumn is pleasant too. Winters are often sunny but can be very cold, with occasional showers, snowfall and freezing winds along the Bosphorus. Summers are hot and sticky, and even Istanbulis get out of town if they can.

Istanbul's most elegant mosque, the Sultanahmet Camii, with its distinctive six minarets

More Numbers
If you ask an Istanbuli how many mosques there are he will probably sigh and tell you that no one has ever managed to count them all. One resident told us there was a mosque for every street, 'and there are many streets'. There are three bridges over the Golden Horn and two over the Bosphorus; a third is planned.

7

Essence of Istanbul

Straddling two continents, a bridge between East and West, Istanbul is a city like no other. Overlooking the Sea of Marmara, it is divided into three major areas by the inlet of the Golden Horn (Haliç) and the straits of the Bosphorus (Boğaziçi). The old city of 'Stambul' offers a taste of the Orient with its thousand and one mosques, steaming *hamamı* (Turkish baths), sublime churches and sensuous bazaars. Across the Karaköy Bridge there is the European face of Istanbul, the districts of Galata and Taksim, where medieval and Ottoman monuments lie between seedy or funky bars, elegant shopping galleries and the best patisseries in town. Facing both old and new, on the Asian shore of the Bosphorus is Üsküdar, now a bustling part of town with many Ottoman mosques.

Below: *feeding the birds in Istanbul*
Bottom: *a bustling scene in the Covered Bazaar*

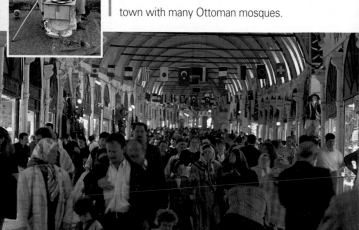

THE 10 ESSENTIALS

There is never enough time to see it all. Here are some essentials:

Left: *many of the old beautiful yalıs along the Bosphorus are now being restored to their former glory*

• **Visit the Topkapı Sarayı** and be intrigued by the Harem, or dazzled by the 86-carat Spoonmaker's Diamond and the Topkapı Dagger (➤ 24–5 and 72–3).

• **See Istanbul** from the panoramic terrace of the old Galata Kulesi (➤ 50) – a great way to understand the city's complicated layout.

• **Cruise on the Bosphorus** (➤ 19 and 83) past beautiful old yalıs (wooden mansions), splendid palaces (➤ 36, 45) and Ottoman fortresses (➤ 32, 65).

• **Indulge yourself** in a Turkish bath. Enjoy a massage and scrub, and come out cleaner than you've ever felt before (➤ 43, 113).

• **Have your wish come true** by turning your thumb full circle in the hole of the famous sweating column in Aya Sofya (➤ 18).

• **Smoke a waterpipe, sip a Turkish coffee** and meditate in writer Piyer Loti's café in Eyüp (➤ 97) or in Café Rumeli, in the peaceful cemetery beside the Atık Ali Paşa Camii (➤ 33).

• **Get lost** in the Kapalıçarşı, or Covered Bazaar (it has 4,000 shops ➤ 20).

• **Take the old tramway back to Taksim Meydanı** after shopping along bustling İstiklâl Caddesi (➤ 53).

Below: *Istanbul from the top of Galata Tower*

• **Angle for a fish from Galata Bridge** or join Istanbulis in one of the many excellent fish restaurants in Kumkapı or along the Bosphorus (➤ 95).

• **Marvel at the brilliance of Sinan**, Süleyman the Magnificent's architect, by visiting some of the hamamı, tombs and 42 mosques (cami) that he built here, starting with his masterpiece, the Süleymaniye Camii (➤ 22).

The Shaping of Istanbul

c40000 BC
Shifting continental plates create the Bosphorus Strait (Boğaziçi), separating Europe and Asia.

c3000 BC
Earliest-known

western European shore. This is where he builds Byzantium.

667 BC–AD 330
Byzantium becomes the richest and most important Greek colony

11 May 330
Emperor Constantine moves the imperial capital from Rome to Byzantium, enlarging it and renaming it Constantinople.

391
Theodosius I declares Christianity the state religion.

527–565
The reign of Justinian the Great and his wife Theodora, who build great palaces and churches, including the Aya Sofya.

Above: *Constantinople, jewel of the empire*

settlement at Chalcedon (Kadıköy) on the Asian shore.

c1400 BC
Small Mycenaean trading post on the peninsula in the Sea of Marmara, now crowned by the Topkapı Sarayı.

667 BC
The Delphic Oracle orders Megaran (Greek) King Byzas to build a town opposite the 'Land of the Blind'. Byzas decides that the Chalcedonians must be blind not to realise the possibilities of the Golden Horn harbour on the

on the Bosphorus, continually threatened by invasion from neighbouring powers: Persia, Sparta, Athens, Macedonia, Celtia and Boetia.

6th century BC
Persian King Darius I builds a bridge over the Bosphorus between Byzantium and Chalcedon.

2nd century AD
When Rome conquers Byzantium, Emperor Septimius Severus destroys the city and massacres its population. He subsequently rebuilds the city twice the size of the original.

610
The empire is almost lost, but Heraclius saves the city from invading armies from Persia and the Balkans.

726–843
Iconoclastic crisis leads to the complete destruction of all religious imagery, including frescoes, icons and mosaics.

843–1204
Heroic Age of the Byzantine Empire revives interest in building grand churches and establishing art schools.

1050
Schism between the Western and Eastern Churches.

10

1182
The inhabitants of Constantinople massacre 6,000 Italians in their trading posts on the Bosphorus.

1204
Crusaders of the 4th Crusade sack the city.

1261
Michael Paleologus and the Greeks recapture the city, but the Byzantine Empire is slowly disintegrating.

1453
Turkish Sultan Mehmet II conquers Constantinople, slaughters its citizens and takes away its treasures.

1454
Mehmet II makes Constantinople capital of his Ottoman Empire: the Turks rename it Istanbul.

1509
45 days of earthquakes destroy many monuments.

1520–1566
The reign of Süleyman the Magnificent and the construction of many wonderful mosques by the architect Sinan.

1699
By the Treaty of Carlowitz, the sultan is forced to cede large territories to Russia and Austria.

1703–1730
Decadent reign of the 'Tulip' Sultan Ahmet III, which ends in a revolution of the Janissaries.

1826
The massacre of the Janissaries in the Hippodrome marks the beginning of modernisation.

1853
Sultan Abdülmecit moves the court from Topkapı to the new Dolmabahçe Sarayı.

1877
First Parliament is inaugurated.

1909
'Young Turk' coup deposes Sultan Abdülhamid II.

1919
Allied armies occupy Istanbul.

1920
Kemal Atatürk presides over the first Great National Assembly at Ankara. Beginning of the War of Independence.

1922
Sultanate is abolished.

1923
Atatürk is the first president of Turkey and Ankara becomes capital.

10 Nov 1938
Atatürk dies in Dolmabahçe Sarayı.

1952
Turkey joins NATO.

1974
Turkish invasion of Cyprus.

1983
After a period of military rule, political parties are permitted. Turgut Ozal becomes head of state.

1987
Turkey applies to become a member of the EC (application still pending).

1990
Census counts 7.5 million inhabitants in Istanbul; it is now probably over 12 million.

1995
Opening of new Istanbul Stock Exchange at İstinye on the Bosphorous.

Right: Mustafa Kemal Atatürk, father of modern Turkey

11

Peace & Quiet

The gardens of the Topkapı Sarayı are a wonderful place to relax after seeing its treasures

Heavy traffic, equally heavy pollution and an exploding population have made peace and quiet hard to find in Istanbul. However, although green spaces are in short supply, the courtyards within the numerous mosques and palaces are oases of calm that offer the visitor a peaceful interlude and a bit of shade. There are also many beautiful cemeteries (➤ 75), usually overgrown and abandoned, where Istanbulis like to stroll, and after a visit to Topkapı Sarayı (➤ 24, 73) it is well worth taking time to explore the gardens, especially for the views over the city. Finally, many areas in the vicinity of Istanbul are fortunately still relatively unspoilt and you don't need to go far to reach lakes or mountains.

Parks and Gardens

The Imperial Rose Garden at Topkapı Sarayı is now a public park, called the Gülhane Parkı (➤ 51), liberally sprinkled with cafés, kiosks and picnic places. The shores of the Golden Horn, scene of extravagant open-air parties and picnics during the Ottoman period, are being restored as a much-needed green zone, with children's playgrounds and benches from which to watch the world go by. The splendid Yıldız Parkı (➤ 78) is a favourite for many, with large areas left to nature, as well as more formal gardens. The well-tended grounds of Beylerbeyi Sarayı (➤ 36) often impress visitors more than the building itself, while on the Asian shore the Fenerbahçe gardens are another peaceful haven – popular with joggers – with excellent views of Sultanahmet.

Birdwatching

Millions of birds migrate over the eastern Mediterranean every spring and autumn and numerous large birds, including eagles, cranes, pelicans and storks, making their way to or from Africa, choose to fly over the Bosphorus rather than larger expanses of sea. It's best to watch them early in the morning from the Çamlıca Hills (Büyük and Küçük Çamlıca), on the Asian shore above Üsküdar. In town, palm doves, several species of swallows and gulls are common, while nightingales, swifts and Orphean warblers may be spotted in secluded gardens. In villages along the Bosphorus you may encounter white storks, which like to nest on rooftops.

Left: *doves inhabit Istanbul's parks and the green areas along the Golden Horn*

Above: *each year over 300,000 storks fly across the Bosphorus on their way to or from Africa*

Lakes and Mountains

On the Asiatic side of the Bosphorus, approximately 160km from the city, there are three large freshwater lakes, equally good for birdwatching and for swimming. The closest to Istanbul is İznik Gölü (Lake İznik), then there is Ulubat Gölü (Lake Apolyont), and the furthest away is Kus Gölü (Lake Manyas). All three lakes are home to herons, egrets, white storks and pelicans. The wetlands on the northeastern shore of Lake Manyas have been protected as the Kuş Cenneti National Park. South of the Sea of Marmara, near Bursa, there is excellent skiing in winter and hiking from spring to autumn on the impressive 2,500m-high Mount Uludağ, or Great Mountain (➤ 90). The Köroğlu Tepe (Mountains), 160km east of Istanbul, also offer very good hiking as well as a glimpse of rural Turkey.

13

Istanbul's Famous

Some of Istanbul's inhabitants or rulers became as legendary and well known as the place itself. From its earliest days the city had a cosmopolitan heart, while the brilliance of its court attracted many artists, writers and travellers.

Legendary Byzantines

Constantine the Great proclaimed the city capital of the Roman Empire in AD 330 in a move to create a Christian capital. By the time he died, Constantinople had become five times bigger than old Byzantium. The Byzantine Empire reached its height during the reign of Justinian (527–65), a great general who brought Spain, parts of Persia, Egypt and some of the Danube lands into the empire. Justinian was also a great builder, and many magnificent palaces and churches, including the Aya Sofya, were commissioned during his lifetime.

Brilliant Ottoman
Sultan Süleyman I (1520–1566) liked to be called *kanuni* or legislator, but Europeans were so impressed by his qualities as a conqueror and ruler as well as legislator that they called him 'the Magnificent'. It was under his rule that the Ottoman Empire reached its apogee. Süleyman broke with Ottoman tradition and honoured his Russian-born wife Roxelana by moving the Harem into his palace. He was a respected poet and an astute patron of the arts.

Above: *Sultan Süleyman the Magnificent*

Below: *Frenchman Pierre Loti who fell in love with the city*

Mustafa Kemal Atatürk

The Ottoman sultanate was abolished on 1 November 1922, and when the Republic of Turkey was founded the following year, Mustafa Kemal was its first president. He was acclaimed as Atatürk, Father of the Turks, for his role in modernising the country. Some of his drastic reforms included the banning of the Arabic script in favour of Latin script and the removal of the capital from Istanbul, which had been the imperial capital for sixteen centuries, to Ankara. Antique clocks in every museum in Turkey stand still at the time he died in 1938, in Istanbul's Dolmabahçe Sarayı.

Visiting Writers

Lady Mary Wortley-Montagu (1689–1762) lived in Istanbul between 1716 and 1718 as the British ambassador's wife and she later wrote of her stay in her volume of *Letters*. Lord Byron (1788–1824), who briefly passed through on his travels, was delighted by the city. Frenchman Pierre Loti stirred the imagination of many of his contemporaries with his celebrated Orientalist novel *Aziyade*, based on his tragic love affair with a harem girl, while his compatriot Gustave Flaubert (1821–80) wrote home about the city's streets and the brothels. Graham Greene's first commercially successful novel was *Stamboul Train* (1932), but the writer who did most for the city was Agatha Christie (1890–1976), whose *Murder on the Orient Express* ends in Istanbul.

Top Ten

Above: *frieze from the Arkeoloji Müzesi*
Right: *a bust on display at the Arkeolji Müzesi*

15

1
Arkeoloji Müzesi
(Archaeological Museum)

 39E3

 Sultanahmet, Gülhane, next door to Topkapı Sarayı

☎ 520 77 40

Archaeological Museum: Tue–Sun 9:30–4:30. Closed Mon. Çinili Köşkü: Fri 9:30–5 only. Museum of the Ancient Orient: alternate days. Closed lunchtime. The main Archaeological Museum is currently undergoing a much-needed reorganisation but remains open to the public.

 Cafeteria (£)

 Tram stop Sultanahmet, Gülhane

 Eminönü İskelesi

 Few

 Moderate

 At Meydanı (➤ 17), Aya Sofya (➤ 18), Topkapı Sarayı (➤ 24–5)

? Video of Anatolia's history daily at 10, 11:30, 1:30 and 3:30. On weekends: children's workshops, children's area with a wooden horse of Troy to climb in.

Right: *a statue from the rich collection of treasures in the Museum of the Ancient Orient*

A remarkable national collection that includes a magnificent sarcophagus from Sidon, a gallery of classical sculptures, and the superb Çinili Köşkü.

Left of the entrance, on the ground floor, look at the exceptional display of sarcophagi, which includes some of the museum's major exhibits. The finest is the 4th-century BC so-called 'Alexander Sarcophagus', discovered in Sidon (Syria). It was made for a Seleucid or Phoenician prince, although Alexander the Great is represented wearing his lion-skin head dress both in a battle scene between Persians and Greeks and in a hunting scene. The 4th-century BC 'Sarcophagus of the Mourning Women' shows 18 women mourning for their King Straton, who died in 360 BC; its Ionic architectural elements are echoed in the façade of the museum itself. To the right of the entrance are the classical sculpture galleries: sculpture covering the period from 800 BC to AD 400 is beautifully displayed and clearly explained. The first-floor gallery runs through the history of Anatolia, from the introduction of agriculture and bronze-making around 10,000 BC to the Lydian and Phrygian kingdoms around 546 BC. Watch the video for the inside story.

Housed in the Museum of the Ancient Orient is a splendid but badly lit and dusty collection of Mesopotamian, Egyptian and Hittite Anatolian artefacts. Look out here for the world's oldest-known peace treaty, the 1269 BC Treaty of Kadesh agreed between the Egyptian Pharaoh Ramses II and the Hittite King Muvatellish. Also of note is the 6th-century BC faience animal relief from the processional way in Babylon.

The 15th-century Çinili Köşkü (Tiled Pavilion) is Istanbul's oldest secular Islamic building. A former royal hunting lodge decorated with calligraphy and turquoise tiles, it now houses a fine collection of Seljuk pottery and İznik tiles.

2
At Meydanı (Hippodrome)

Most of Constantinople's resplendent cultural heart is gone, but the garden square, with Sultanahmet Camii and Aya Sofya on either side, still impresses.

Below and left: *the 16th-century BC Egyptian Obelisk*

The Hippodrome race track was built by Emperor Septimius Severus in the 2nd century AD, and enlarged by Constantine the Great to a length of 480m. Today's road around the square follows the track exactly, but the amphitheatre was destroyed to build the Sultanahmet Camii (► 23). To the east stood the imperial enclosure (Kathisma), which was connected to the palace of the Byzantine emperors. The Ottomans pulled down many monuments around the Hippodrome, but it remained the place where state ceremonies and executions were performed. The tourist office stands on the site of a tower once crowned by the famous bronze horses of San Marco, Venice, looted by the Venetians during the 4th Crusade.

The Egyptian Obelisk, of the Pharaoh Thutmose III (1504–1450 BC) commemorating his Syrian campaign, was brought to Constantinople in the 4th century. Originally 60m tall, it broke during shipment and only the top third was mounted on a marble base decorated with an image of Theodosius I and his family in the Kathisma, watching scenes in the Hippodrome. The 5th-century BC Serpent Column, with three intertwined bronze snakes, was brought from the Apollo Temple at Delphi by Constantine the Great. A third monument, the Column of Constantine Porphyrogenitus, bears an inscription to the effect that it was restored and sheathed in gold-plated bronze, which disappeared during the sack of Constantinople in 1204. The elegant fountain near the Aya Sofya was a gift to Sultan Abdülhamid II from Kaiser Wilhelm II, an admirer.

✠ 39D2

✉ At Meydanı, Sultanahmet

🍴 Darüzziyafe restaurant (££) (► 92)

🚌 Tram stop Sultanahmet

ℹ Tourist office
☎ 518 87 54

♿ Good

✋ Free

↔ Aya Sofya (► 18), Sultanahmet Camii (► 23), Yerebatan Sarayı (► 26), Divan Yolu (► 44), Roxelana Hamamı (► 64), Türk ve İslam Eserleri Müzesi (► 74)

❓ Re-creation of traditional life with Karagöz tent, tea houses and Ramazan specialities during the month of Ramazan

17

3

Aya Sofya (Church of the Divine Wisdom)

✝ 39E2

✉ Aya Sofya Meydanı, Sultanahmet

🕐 Tue–Sun 9–4 (Galleries 9–3:30). Closed Mon

🍴 Cafeteria (£) just outside the compound

🚌 Tram stop Sultanahmet

♿ Good (none for galleries)

✋ Moderate

↔ Arkeoloji Müzesi (► 16), At Meydanı (► 17), Sultanahmet Camii (► 23), Topkapı Sarayı (► 24–5), Yerebatan Sarayı (► 26), Roxelana Hamamı (► 64)

The splendid Aya Sofya

When inaugurating the Aya Sofya, Justinian declared: 'O Solomon, I surpassed you'. His achievement remains an object of wonder.

Looking at the stern exterior, with its buttresses and minarets, it is hard to understand how this building was the inspiration for Roman cathedrals and for Mimar Sinan's extraordinary mosques; but inside, the building's perfect harmony and grandeur is astounding. Now regarded as an icon of the Byzantine Empire, Aya Sofya was inaugurated in 537 by Justinian, converted into a mosque a few hours after the Ottoman conquest in 1453, and became a museum in the 20th century.

The church was designed as a basilica around a basic rectangular plan, the centre of which is covered by the building's touch of genius, a truly massive dome, the largest known in antiquity. (The calligraphic inscription in its centre is a mid-19th-century addition.) The central Imperial Door, crowned by a fine mosaic of Emperor Leo VI before Christ, was once reserved for the emperor and leads to the impressive narthex. To the extreme right is the Vestibule of Warriors (or exit) with an exquisite mosaic of

Constantine and Justinian offering models of the Aya Sofya and Constantinople to Christ and the Virgin. The stairway to the left leads to the galleries.

The scale of the nave is quite overwhelming, and it takes time to get used to it. The immense space is lit by 40 windows in the dome, the walls and pillars are clad in rare marbles, and the ceiling has retained gold mosaics (admire them at close quarters from the upper galleries). Some of the most beautiful of the mosaics that once covered the greater part of the walls can be seen in the south gallery. These, like all the other figurative mosaics, date from after the end of the Iconoclastic period (730–843), during which the portrayal of humans had been banned. The so-called sweating column, near the gallery stairway, is believed to heal illnesses, in particular infertility.

4
Boğaziçi
(Bosphorus)

Take a relaxing cruise up the Bosphorus, admiring newly restored yalıs (summer mansions), sumptuous palaces and impressive castles.

Galata Bridge links Europe and Asia

The 16th-century French scholar Petrus Gyllius described the 35km-long Bosphorus as the 'strait that surpasses all straits, because with one key it opens and closes two worlds, two seas'. The Bosphorus connects the Black Sea with the Sea of Marmara, and divides Europe from Asia. Between the villages of Bebek and Kuleli, where the Bosphorus reaches its maximum depth (about 100m), are dangerous currents known as the 'Currents of the Devil'.

The strait has always been strategically important: in 1452, using the twin castles of Anadolu (➤ 32) and Rumeli Hisarı (➤ 65), the Ottoman conqueror Mehmet cut off the city's food supply. At Anadolu Kavağı, at the Black Sea end, Byzantine fortifications survive. In times of peace, sultans would escape to their waterfront pleasure palaces in elegant caiques, now in the Deniz Müzesi (➤ 44).

The two surviving imperial palaces on the Bosphorus are the 19th-century Beylerbeyi Sarayı (➤ 36) and the Dolmabahçe Sarayı (➤ 45), the imperial court's last home. A string of picturesque yalıs (summer mansions) and some fast-developing fishing villages line the shores. Sarıyer (➤ 90), on the European shore of the upper Bosphorus, is particularly worth visiting for its harbour, fish restaurants and the Sadberk Hanım Müzesi (➤ 66), a wonderful 19th-century yalı with a great collection of antique and Ottoman art. Unfortunately, the Bosphorus now suffers from an increasing number of large high-speed tankers, which create powerful waves on the otherwise still waters and pose a significant threat to the palaces and mansions. (See also map ➤ 82 and cruise/drive ➤ 83.)

✚ 82B5

🍴 See restaurant section (➤ 98–9)

🚌 Dolmuş from Taksim for European side, from Üsküdar on the Asian side

⛴ Ferries from Beşiktaş and Eminönü (panel ➤ 83)

♿ None

✋ Cheap

↔ Anadolu Hisarı (➤ 32), Beylerbeyi Sarayı (➤ 36), Deniz Müzesi (➤ 44), Dolmabahçe Sarayı (➤ 45), Ortaköy Camii (➤ 63), Rumeli Hisarı (➤ 65), Sadberk Hanım Müzesi (➤ 66), Selimiye Kışlası (➤ 67), Üsküdar (➤ 74–5), Sarıyer (➤ 90)

❓ During the first full moon (Mehtap) of autumn, fishermen go fishing for schools of small bluefish.

5

Kapalıçarşı
(Covered Bazaar)

Bargain hard is the motto in the Covered Bazaar

One of the largest and most famous covered markets in the world, the Kapalıçarşı still lures visitors into the world of 1,001 nights.

✚ 38C3

✉ Beyazıt

🕐 Mon–Sat 9–7. Closed Sun

🍴 Havuzlu (➤ 93)

🚌 Tram stop Beyazıt

♿ Few

🆓 Free

↔ Beyazıt Camii (➤ 34), Beyazıt Meydanı (➤ 35), Çemberlitaş (➤ 43), Çorlulu Ali Paşa Külliyesi (➤ 43), Mahmut Paşa Camii (➤ 57), Mısır Çarşısı (➤ 59), Nuruosmaniye Camii (➤ 62), Rüstem Paşa Camii (➤ 65)

❓ Auctions: Tue (furniture), Wed (carpets), Thu (jewellery)

A labyrinth of 4,000 shops, workshops, stalls, *hans* (caravanserais), restaurants and tea houses, the Covered (or Grand) Bazaar is a unique trading area, employing over 20,000 people selling whatever there is to be sold. The market was built by the order of Fatih Mehmet II shortly after the Conquest, but has been rebuilt several times after fires, most recently in the 1950s. The plan and the structure are basically as they were in the early Ottoman years. As then, so today streets still tend to sell one particular product, although shops selling Western clothes and tourist tat are spreading fast throughout the bazaar.

At first the bazaar can be a bewildering place, but the main thoroughfares (including Yaglıkçılar Caddesi, Halıcılar Caddesi and Kesecıler Caddesi) soon become familiar. The two original *bedestens* or warehouses survive at the heart of the bazaar. The most precious goods – such as antiques and jewellery – are stored at the İç Bedesten, or Old Bedesten, a rectangular building with 15 domes dating from the time of Mehmet II. The nearby Sandal Bedesten, dating from the time of Süleyman and covered with 20 domes, is now the venue for auctions. The vaulted Halıcılar Caddesi has clusters of the best carpet dealers, while the wider Kalpakçılar Caddesi is home to the majority of jewellers and gold shops.

6
Kariye Camii
(St Saviour in Chora)

The former church of St Saviour in Chora glitters with some of the finest mosaics to be found in any Byzantine church in the world.

'In Chora' means 'in the country', as the original St Saviour Church stood outside the Constantinian walls and was only later enclosed by the Theodosian Walls. The present church, erected in 1081, was converted into a mosque more than 50 years after the Ottoman conquest by Grand Vizier Atık Ali Paşa, and is now a museum. The mosaics, which were damaged by earthquakes, covered with paint or plaster and finally restored to their original splendour by the Byzantine Institute of America, rank among the world's most important examples of Byzantine pictorial art.

The portrait over the entrance to the nave is of Theodore Metochites, the man who commissioned these mosaics in the 14th century. In contrast to the static and stylised work of the earlier Byzantine period, these are notable for their directness and realism. The luminous vitality of the colours gives the scenes a sense of lightness and spirituality. The mosaics fall into seven groups: six large dedicatory images in the narthex and exonarthex; the Ancestry of Christ in the domes of the inner narthex; Cycle of Life of the Blessed Virgin in the first three bays of the inner narthex; Cycle of Infancy of Christ in the lunettes of the outer narthex; Cycle of Christ's Ministry in the vaults of the outer narthex; portraits of saints. The side chapel to the right, the Parekklesion, is decorated with frescoes whose beauty, perfect execution and brilliant colours – particularly the Resurrection – are also amongst the city's greatest treasures.

✚ 28B4

✉ Kariye Camii Sokak 28, Edirnekapı, Fatih

☎ 631 92 41

🕐 9:30–4:30. Closed Tue

🚌 Bus from Eminönü to Edirnekapi

♿ Few

✋ Moderate

↔ Mihrimah Camii (➤ 58), Tekfur Sarayı (➤ 70), Theodosian Walls (➤ 71)

A superb fresco in the apse of the Parekklesion, with Christ pulling Adam and Eve up to Heaven

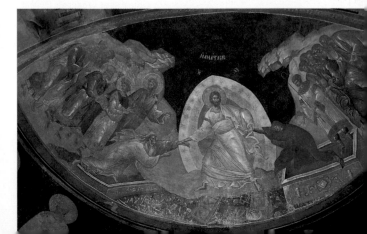

7
Süleymaniye Camii

View of the Süleymaniye Camii from across the Golden Horn

A pearl of classical Ottoman architecture, this mosque surpasses every other in the perfection of its design and the harmony of its decoration.

Built between 1550 and 1557, the majestic Süleymaniye Camii represents the culmination of a lifetime's co-operation between the genial architect Mimar Sinan (► 65) and his generous patron, Sultan Süleyman I. The mosque is approached through the grand colonnaded courtyard, a large open space, edged with marble, granite and porphyry columns, that exudes a sense of peace and harmony. Four slender minarets in the corners of the forecourt are said to mark Süleyman's position as the fourth Ottoman ruler of Istanbul, while ten balconies refer to his position as the tenth ruler since Osman.

The prayer hall, crowned by a magnificent central dome, is notable for the way that embellishment was kept to a minimum in order to set off the exceptionally fine masonry. The *mihrab* arch is sumptuously decorated with some of the most glorious tiles ever produced in İznik, depicting flowers in strong tones of blue and red. The doors and shutters are intricately inlaid with mother-of-pearl and ivory. Coloured light filters through superb stained-glass windows.

The *türbe* (mausoleum) of Süleyman lies in the overgrown garden behind the mosque. Appropriately, it is the grandest of the mausoleums designed by Sinan, with a double dome (one of Sinan's signature touches) and it too is decorated with superb İznik tiles. The *türbe* of Roxelana, Süleyman's wife, is smaller, but the decoration is even more impressive, the tiles even finer. Sinan's tomb is by comparison a modest affair, located in the northern corner of the square. There are superb views over the courtyards of the rest of the complex, including several schools, a mental asylum, public kitchen, bazaar, *hamamı* (baths), caravanserai and a medical college.

✚ 38B4

✉ Süleymaniye

🕓 Dawn to dusk

🚌 Tram stop Beyazıt

♿ None

👆 Free; tip the man who guards the shoes

↔ Beyazıt Camii (► 34), Beyazıt Meydanı (► 35), Rüstem Paşa Camii (► 65)

8
Sultanahmet Camii
(The Blue Mosque)

The Sultanahmet Camii, also known as the Blue Mosque, is recognisable on Istanbul's skyline: it is the only dome surrounded by six minarets.

This bubble bath in stone, a remarkable series of domes and semi-domes percolating between six slender, fluted minarets, is often considered one of the architectural wonders of the world. The mosque was completed in 1616, built for Sultan Ahmet I by Mehmet Ağa, a pupil of Sinan. The four minarets on the corners of the courtyard have three decorative balconies (*şerefes*), the others have two – making 16 in all, from each of which a muezzin used to call for prayer. Several monumental gateways lead into the mosque and although tourists are asked to enter via the side gate, individuals are allowed to enter through the main gate, as the sultan's procession used to do after the Friday call to prayer – a much more spectacular approach. The vast courtyard, bordered by a portico with 30 domes and with an elegant ablution fountain at the centre, is perfectly in proportion with the grand scale of the mosque itself.

The vast interior (53m wide, 51m long) is covered by a huge dome supported on all sides by semi-domes which are, in turn, supported by smaller domes. Light floods in through 250 windows that were once filled with coloured glass. The Sultanahmet Camii is called the Blue Mosque after the exquisite floral-patterned İznik tiles – there are over 20,000 – that cover the lower part of the walls. From the prime period late in the 16th century, they feature the traditional lilies, tulips, carnations and roses in subtle shades of blue and green. The upper part is painted in rather crude modern designs. Note the delicate carving on the early 17th-century white marble *mihrab* and *mimbar*.

Istanbulis enter the Blue Mosque from the main gateway, with great views of its domes and cupolas

23

9
Topkapı Sarayı
(Topkapı Palace)

The sumptuous palace, the intrigues of the Harem and the wonders of the Imperial Treasures bring to life the splendours of the Ottoman Empire.

39F3

Sultanahmet behind the Aya Sofya (for ground-plan of the museum ➤ 72)

512 04 80

Wed–Mon. Closed Tue. Palace: 9:30–5:30. Harem: 10–3:30

Konyalı Restaurant (£££) & Cafeteria (£–££) (➤ 93)

Tram stop Sultanahmet

Very good

Moderate (separate ticket for Harem needs to be booked as soon as you arrive as the daily numbers are limited: moderate)

Arkeoloji Müzesi (➤ 16), At Meydanı (➤ 17), Aya Sofya (➤ 18), Sultanahmet Camii (➤ 23), Ahmet III Çeşmesi (➤ 32), Aya İrini Kilise (➤ 34), Caferağa Medrese (➤ 41), Gülhane Parkı (➤ 51)

Harem: guided tour only

In 1461 Mehmet the Conqueror ordered the construction of the Topkapı Sarayı (also ➤ 72–3), his governmental palace, on the site of the Greek colony of Byzantium and in a perfect location on the Bosphorus, overlooking both the Sea of Marmara and the Golden Horn. When the imperial residence in Beyazıt burned down in 1541 (➤ 35), Süleyman the Magnificent moved his residence to Topkapı – a bad move, as it turned out, for both family and state affairs became riddled with intrigues. The palace was constantly added to and embellished until it finally housed more than 5,000 people. In 1855 Sultan Abdülmecit moved the imperial household to the Dolmabahçe Sarayı (➤ 45), and in 1924 Kemal Atatürk opened Topkapı as a museum.

The impressive Bab-ı Hümayun, the main entrance to the palace, leads into the First Court or the Court of the Janissaries, who paraded here and used the Aya İrini Kilise (➤ 34), in the southwest corner of the court, as their arsenal. Ortakapı, the Middle Gate, whose imposing twin towers were the home of the imperial executioner, leads into the enormous Second Court, or the Courtyard of the Divan, the Council Chamber from where the Grand Vizier and administrators governed the empire.

Access to the Harem, once protected by black eunuchs, is via the Carriage Gate, next to the Divan. In the labyrinthine rooms of the Harem, the Sultan lived with his extended family in the midst of intrigue, bloodshed and jealousy. Amongst the many breathtaking rooms here, look out for the 'Room with a Hearth', with exceptional faience tiles and bronze fireplace, the Hall of the Emperor, the largest in the palace, and the even more impressive Salon of Murat III, believed to have been created by Sinan and still in its original state, with bronze fireplace, exquisite İznik tiles, calligraphic frieze and a three-tiered marble fountain. Ahmet I's library has tortoiseshell

Brilliantly coloured tiles in Topkapı Sarayı

and mother-of-pearl inlaid cabinets and wonderful views over the Bosphorus, while Ahmet III's dining room with flowers and fruit painted on lacquered wood is typical of the decadent Tulip period. The most notorious rooms in the Harem were the suite known as the Cage, created as an alternative to killing the Sultan's brothers. In the Cage possible rivals were allowed to live in luxurious isolation, often resulting in either debauchery or madness. The location of these rooms remains a matter of speculation.

Left: *Mehmet the Conqueror's Sword*

The Third Courtyard housed the palace schools and chambers where sultans received ministers and foreign ambassadors. To the right, with a domed portico, is the Imperial Costume Collection, exhibiting sumptuous clothing. Beside it, the Pavilion of the Conqueror is home to the dazzling Imperial Treasures, including the Spoonmaker's Diamond, fifth largest in the world, and the emerald-encrusted Topkapı Dagger. Across the courtyard the Pavilion of the Holy Mantle holds several of the most sacred relics in Islam, including a hair and tooth of Prophet Muhammad. The Fourth Courtyard consists of several pavilions: note in particular the beautiful tiling, inside and out, of the Bağdat Köşkü.

Below: *the Harem's richly decorated* Hünkar *or Imperial Chamber*

10
Yerebatan Sarayı
(Underground Palace)

+ 39E2

✉ Yerebatan Caddesi 13, Sultanahmet

☎ 522 12 59

🕐 Daily 9–4:30 (until 7 in summer)

🍴 Cafeteria (£)

🚌 Tram stop Sultanahmet

♿ None

✋ Moderate

↔ At Meydanı (➤ 17), Aya Sofya (➤ 18), Sultanahmet Camii (➤ 23), Caferağa Medrese (➤ 41), Cağaloğlu Hamamı (➤ 41), Divan Yolu (➤ 44)

The columned interior of Yerebatan Sarayı; once filled with water from springs in Belgrade Forest

This spectacular and well-restored Byzantine cistern, the main source of water for Istanbul's First Hill, is one of the city's most eerie sites.

Dark, damp steps lead down to a vast subterranean reservoir, 140m long and 70m wide, where a forest of dramatically lit pillars supports a magnificent arched roof. Originally there were 336 columns, but 90 remain behind a 19th-century wall. They were mostly taken from pagan temples, while the two Medusa heads used as column bases at the back of the chamber probably came from the city of Chalcedon, on the Asian shore, after it was dismantled by Justinian. Walkways lead over the water to the ornamental fountain at the back. Classical music in the background adds to the mystery of the place, with the constant running water adding a refrain of its own.

Believed to have been built by Constantine the Great, the cistern is named in English the Basilica Cistern after the Stoa Basilica, which stood directly above it. The Stoa Basilica was destroyed by fire in 425, and the cistern was rebuilt and enlarged in 532 by Justinian. Used extensively throughout the Byzantine period, it continued in use after the Ottoman conquest, supplying water for the Topkapı Sarayı gardens. Subsequently knowledge of the cistern seems to have been lost to the outside world until a French Byzantine scholar, Petrus Gyllius, investigated tall stories told by locals about fishing in the basement of their houses. He was lowered down a well head, and 're-discovered' what is now called the Underground Palace.

What to See

Above: *Medusa head from the Yerebatan Sarayı*
Right: *red hot chilli peppers*

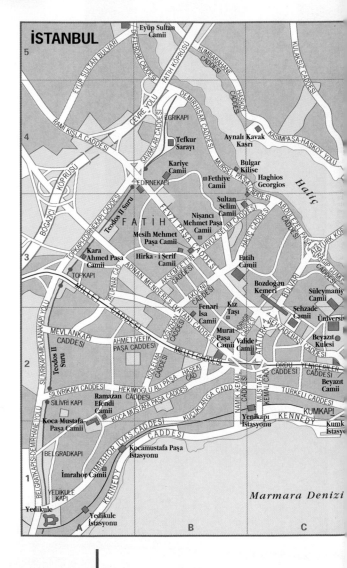

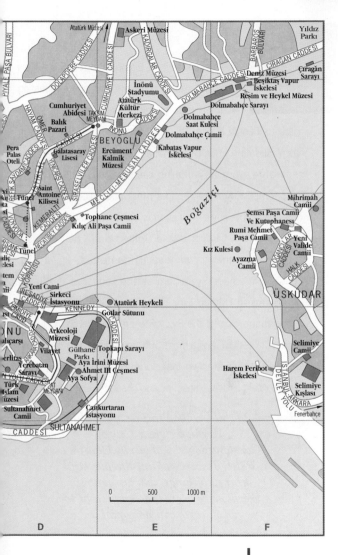

Istanbul

The name says it all: Istanbul, from the Greek *eis tēn polin*, meaning 'in the city' and suggesting that this unforgettable place needs no other name to identify it than 'The City'. Istanbul is unique in that it has placed its feet on two continents, with the European side separated from its suburbs on the Asian side by the Bosphorus, one of the world's most strategically important waterways. The city's position was so advantageous, with the perfect natural harbour of the Golden Horn, that it was a cherished capital for almost 16 centuries. In AD 330, Constantine chose Byzantium as the capital of the newly Christianised Roman Empire and, as Constantinople, it remained the glory of the Byzantine Empire until the Ottoman conquest in 1453. For almost 500 years after the conquest, Ottoman sultans lavished their fortunes on adorning the city with splendid palaces, mosques and charitable institutions.

> ' I beheld… the Prospect of that little
> World, the great City of
> Constantinople… of goodly Churches,
> stately Towers, gallant Steeples, and
> other such things, whereof now the
> World make so great accompt, that the
> whole earth can not equal it. '

EDWARD LITHGOZ
Rare Adventures and Painefull Peregrinations
London, 1640

The City

Istanbul is a city of many layers. The grand monuments around Sultanahmet are so splendid they will easily hold your attention for several days. Crossing the fabled Haliç (Golden Horn) on the Karaköy or Galata Bridge, you enter another old city, a European one, with splendid turn-of-the-century façades and (often) sleazy bars. The Boğaziçi (Bosphorus), busy with an endless succession of boats, is lined with palaces and *yalıs* (wooden mansions), while on the Asian side are yet more stunning mosques.

Many of the major monuments are in the Sultanahmet and Eminönü districts. Within walking distance of each other, chances are between one and the next you will pass a street market, a *medrese* (Islamic school) where you may hear children chanting the verses of the Koran, a tiny mosque, or the tomb of a saint covered in offerings. These street scenes are timeless and exotic, but there is another,

Delicious melon slices for sale in the streets of Istanbul

equally convincing side to the city's character. Enter a bar in Ortaköy or a shopping mall in Etiler and you can imagine yourself in London or New York. Another amazing aspect of Istanbul is the fact that it is constantly growing – indeed, a large part of the city still does not feature on maps. Areas such as Suadiye and Bostancı on the Asian shore of the Marmara Denizi (Sea of Marmara), home to upmarket shops, funky bars and good nightspots, are rarely visited by tourists but are as much a part of the city as the skyline of a thousand minarets. You can see the uniqueness of the city in the faces in the streets – Anatolian peasants and Western tourists, Istanbuli gentlemen and Turkish students, Russian opportunists and Uzbek and Bulgarian tradesmen.

A rare survival of the Tulip period, this fountain is proof of Sultan Ahmet III's excellent taste

What to See in Istanbul

AHMET III ÇEŞMESİ (FOUNTAIN) ✪✪

This elegant fountain, in front of the Bab-ı Hümayun of the Topkapı Sarayı (➤ 24–5), was built in an exquisite rococo style by the Tulip Sultan Ahmet III in 1729. Constantinople was then a place of pleasure and *joie de vivre*, and this fountain is one of the few survivors from that period. Decorated with green and blue tiles and sculptural ornament, it seems to be constantly changing colour. Each corner has a *sebil* (counter), from which fountain attendants served the public with spring water or *sherbets* in silver cups. The verses decorating the upper part, written by the poet Seyit Vehbi Efendi, reveal the construction date in alphabetical notation.

ANADOLU HİSARI ✪

Built by Sultan Beyazıt I in 1390, the small Anadolu Hisarı (Anatolian Castle) looks across the narrowest part of the Bosphorus to its much grander counterpart, the Rumeli Hisarı (➤ 65). A stairway leads to the keep, now a meeting place of local drunks, and from the walls there are great views across the strait. The rivers below the castle, the Göksu Deresi and the Küçüksu, were known to early European travellers as 'the Sweet Waters of Asia'. They were favourite picnic spots for the Ottoman nobility. It is possible to rent small boats for rowing on the streams or for exploring the Bosphorus.

39E2
Bab-ı Hümayun Caddesi, in front of the entrance to Topkapı Sarayı, Sultanahmet
Tram stop Sultanahmet
Good
Free
Aya Sofya (➤ 18), Topkapı Sarayı (➤ 24–5), Aya İrini Kilise (➤ 34)

82C3
Asian shore of the lower Bosphorus, 6km beyond the Bosphorus Bridge
Not officially open but possible to climb up
Small café terrace with snacks and drinks (£)
Bus from Çengelköy
None
Free
Küçüksu Kasrı (➤ 56)

ARKEOLOJİ MÜZESİ (ARCHAEOLOGICAL MUSEUM)
(► 16, TOP TEN)

ASKERİ MÜZESİ (MILITARY MUSEUM) ✪

The museum is divided between newly arranged displays of ancient cannons, weapons and uniforms, and a sumptuous shrine devoted to the national heroes of Turkey. In the latter part note the wonderful embroidered tents from the Ottoman campaigns, a collection of miniature Janissary costumes and the Byzantine chain that sealed the Golden Horn. The main attraction, however, is the performance of the Janissary marching band that takes place outside the museum. The Mehter Band, founded in 1289, soon became a symbol of the power of the Ottoman Empire. Janissaries accompanied the sultan into war, singing rousing songs about battle victories and Ottoman heroes. Their fame spread as far as Europe, where they influenced numerous composers, including Mozart and Beethoven. The Janissaries were abolished in 1826 by Sultan Mahmut II, but were re-established in 1914.

✚ 29E5
✉ Cumuriyet Caddesi, Harbiye
☎ 233 71 15
🕐 Wed–Sun 9–5. Closed Mon, Tue
🍴 None
♿ None
▥ Moderate
↔ Taksim Meydanı (► 70)
❓ Summer: daily performances of the Janissary band. Winter: check with tourist office or ticket office

Below: *Janissaries still perform traditional songs*

ATATÜRK MÜZESİ ✪

Atatürk, the much-loved founder of modern Turkey, and his family lived briefly in this three-storey house, just before the 1919 revolution. The house displays some of his personal effects, original letters and photographs – mainly of interest to devoted Atatürk fans and historians.

✚ 29E5
✉ Halaskârgazi Caddesi 250, Şişli
🕐 9:30–12 and 1–4:30. Closed Thu, Sun
▥ Cheap

ATIK ALİ PAŞA CAMİİ ✪

This small mosque, beside Çemberlitaş, or the Column of Constantine (► 43), is one of the oldest in the city, built in 1496 by the Eunuch Ali Paşa, who was Grand Vizier of Beyazıt II. The mosque was also known as the Mosque of the Workers in Mother-of-Pearl, because it was once surrounded by their workshops. The central hall of the mosque is interesting for the unusual division of its space, beneath a central dome and a further half-dome above the *mihrab*. Note the beautifully carved stone squinches beneath the half-dome and the smaller cupolas.

✚ 38C2
✉ Yeniçeriler Caddesi, Sultanahmet
🕐 During prayer hours
🚊 Tram stop Sultanahmet
♿ None
▥ Free
↔ Kapalıçarşı (► 20), Çemberlitaş (► 43), Nuruosmaniye Camii (► 62)

AT MEYDANI (HIPPODROME) (➤ 17, TOP TEN)

AYA İRİNİ KİLİSE ✪✪ (THE CHURCH OF DIVINE PEACE)

Built in the early 4th century, this is the second largest Byzantine church in Istanbul (Aya Sofya is the largest) and one of the oldest. Excavations beneath the church revealed the remains of earlier temples to Aphrodite and other Roman gods. Unlike most of Istanbul's churches, Aya İrini was never converted into a mosque; until the 19th century it was used as a military arsenal for the Topkapı Sarayı. It housed a Military Museum from 1919 until 1946 and now, after an excellent restoration, is a venue for concerts and special exhibitions.

Aya İrini was built as a domed basilica, with two rows of columns and three naves. Most of the original mosaic decoration has disappeared, revealing impressive brickwork, particularly the vaults supporting the dome in the central nave. A mosaic of a cross against a golden background remains in the apse, probably part of the original decoration. The apse also contains the only surviving *synthronon* (seating for the clergy) in the city. The overall effect of the interior inspires deep spirituality. At the western end of the church are five doors which lead to the only surviving Byzantine courtyard in Istanbul, now filled with old tombs.

AYA SOFYA (➤ 18, TOP TEN)

BALKAPANI HANI (HAN OF THE HONEY STORE) ✪✪

The neighbourhood behind the mosque of Rüstem Paşa (➤ 65) still counts several ancient *hans* or caravanserais that date back to Byzantine times. The buildings of the Balkapanı Hanı are Ottoman but the courtyard is original. Stairs in the middle of this busy courtyard lead down to impressive original Byzantine storage places. Today, as ever, they are used to house imported goods, though instead of honey that now means toys made in China. Ask one of the workmen to take you underground.

BEYAZIT CAMİİ ✪✪✪

Beyazıt Camii is the oldest surviving imperial mosque in Istanbul. This exceptional building remains a perfect example of classical Ottoman architecture.

➕ 39E2
✉ First Courtyard of Topkapı Sarayı, Sultanahmet
🕐 Open only when used for exhibitions or concerts
🚊 Tram stop Sultanahmet
♿ Few
✋ Free
↔ Arkeoloji Müzesi (➤ 16), Topkapı Sarayı (➤ 24–5), Ahmet III Çeşmesi (➤ 32)
❓ Check with tourist office for dates of concerts and exhibitions

The interior of the Beyazıt Camii is a smaller version of the Aya Sofya

➕ 38C4
✉ Balkapanı Sokak, off Hasırcılar Caddesi, Eminönü
🕐 Shop hours. Closed on Sun
♿ None
↔ Süleymaniye Camii (➤ 22), Mısır Çarşısı (➤ 59)

➕ 38C2
✉ Beyazıt Meydanı
🕐 Hours of prayer

Built in 1501–5 by Beyazıt II, son of the Conqueror Mehmet II, on the same plan as the Aya Sofya, it has one massive central dome and two side half-domes. The sultan's *loge* (a raised seat) is supported by wonderful marble columns. The courtyard is one of the most beautiful in the city, with a pavement of multicoloured marble and arcades resting on ancient porphyry and Syenite columns with Islamic capitals. The minarets are inlaid with red stone and decorated with Kufic script. Beside the cafés a gate leads to an enclosed garden and the elegant domed tomb of Sultan Beyazıt.

Ⓧ Café-terraces beside the mosque (£)
Ⓧ Tram stop Beyazıt
Ⓧ Few
Ⓧ Free
Ⓧ Kapalıçarşı (➤ 20), Çorlulu Ali Paşa Külliyesi (➤ 43)

BEYAZIT MEYDANI   ✪✪

This busy square near the Kapalıçarşı, or Covered Bazaar (➤ 20), is overlooked by the old Beyazıt Camii (➤ 35) and the attractive Moorish-style gateway to Istanbul University. Besides being an open-air market where tiny stalls sell cheap knick-knacks, the square is also a popular meeting place for students, some traditionally veiled in *chadors*, others wearing the latest high street fashions. In the theological college opposite the mosque is a small Museum of Calligraphy. The university, built on the site of the palace of Mehmet the Conqueror, which burned down in 1541, still exudes an air of splendour and importance. The Beyazıt Tower, a fire tower situated in the courtyard of the university, can be seen from across the city.

Ⓧ 38B3
Ⓧ Officially called Hürriyet Meydanı (Freedom Square), Beyazıt
Ⓧ Museum of Calligraphy: Tue–Sat 9–4
Ⓧ Cafés (£)
Ⓧ Tram stop Beyazıt
Ⓧ Few
Ⓧ Free
Ⓧ Kapalıçarşı (➤ 20), Beyazıt Camii (➤ 34), Divan Yolu (➤ 44)

35

82B2
Çayirbaşi Duraği Beylerbeyi, Asian shore of the Bosphorus
216 321 93 20
9:30–4 for guided tours only. Closed Mon, Thu
In summer café in the garden (£)
From quay no.1 in Eminönü to Üsküdar, then bus no.15
None
Expensive
Üsküdar (➤ 74–5)

The interior of Beylerbeyi Sarayı doesn't appeal to all tastes, but it never fails to impress

BEYLERBEYİ SARAYI (PALACE OF THE LORD OF LORDS) ★★

Now dwarfed by the Bosphorus (Boğaziçi) Bridge, this large marble palace was built in a record four years, between 1861 and 1865, as a summer palace for Sultan Abdülaziz (1861–76). During construction the sultan apparently employed 400 musicians to encourage his workers to greater efforts. Set in magnificent gardens, the palace is enormous (over 3,000sq m), and although the exterior is purely European, the traditional Ottoman divide between the harem and the *selamlık* (men's area) was respected.

Most of the palace's original, opulent furnishings are retained, including heavy Bohemian and Venetian chandeliers, Chinese porcelain vases, French gilt furniture and Turkish carpets. Kitchens and other services occupied the ground floor, from which the main staircase sweeps majestically up to the six impressive salons and 20 other chambers of the two upper floors. The dining chairs in the harem and *selamlık* were carved by Sultan Abdul Hamid II, who was imprisoned here from 1912 to 1918.

39D2
Binbirdirek Meydanı, at the end of Işık Sokak, Sultanahmet
Tram stop Sultanahmet
Yerebatan Sarayı (➤ 26), Çemberlitaş (➤ 43), Divan Yolu (➤ 44)

BİNBİRDİREK SARNIÇ (CISTERN) ★★

The second largest Byzantine cistern in the city (it has 224 columns – not 1,001 as its name indicates), Binbirdirek is currently being renovated as a market place for tourists. The cistern is probably of 5th-century date, although the 4th-century AD Roman Senator Philoxenes, who accompanied Emperor Constantine I into the city, is usually credited with building it. It dried up in the 15th century and in the Ottoman era was used as a spinning mill.

Beyazıt & Kapalıçarşı (Covered Bazaar)

Start at the Süleymaniye Camii (► 22).

After the visit follow the walls of the university to the left, past several campuses, to Beyazıt Meydanı (► 35).

The contrast in appearance between the students and people in the nearby bazaars is very striking. Walk through the university's Moorish-style gateway to the 19th-century Beyazıt Tower for good views from the upper gallery.

Return to the square.

Go into the courtyard of Beyazıt Camii (► 35) and walk out the other side, past the café terraces to the left. From here a passage leads into the delightful book market, Sahaflar Çarşısı.

Walk through to the end and cross Çadırcılar Caddesi. To the right is an entrance to the Covered Bazaar (► 20), Fesçiler Caddesi.

Further to the left is Havuzlu restaurant (► 93) and Şark Kahvesi, where you can sit at an outside table and watch the world go by.

Turn left on Yağcılar Caddesi and then first right, Halıcılar Caddesi.

Some of the best rugs in the market are sold here.

At Fes Café (► 97) turn left into the Old Bazaar. Walk straight across, continuing to the third crossroads, Kalpakçılar Caddesi, the bazaar's main thoroughfare. Turn left and leave the bazaar by the Nuruosmaniye Gate. Turn right, and right again along Tavukpazarı Sokağı to Çemberlitaş, or the Column of Constantine (► 43).

Next to the column is the Vezir Hanı, once the city's main slave market, and the Çemberlitaş Hamamı, where you might stop for a relaxing bath and massage.

The university and Beyazıt Tower, where old concubines of the sultan ended their days

Distance
Approx 2km

Time
3–4 hours (more if you get involved in shopping), and 1–2 hours for the *hamam*

Start point
⊞ 38B4
🚇 Beyazıt

End point
⊞ 39D2
🚇 Sultanahmet

Refreshment
Lunch at Havuzlu (£) (► 93), a Turkish coffee at Şark Cafe on Yağcılar Caddesi, or a cappuccino in Fes Café (► 97)

🚇 Çemberlitaş Hamamı
(££) ✉ Vezirhan Caddesi 8

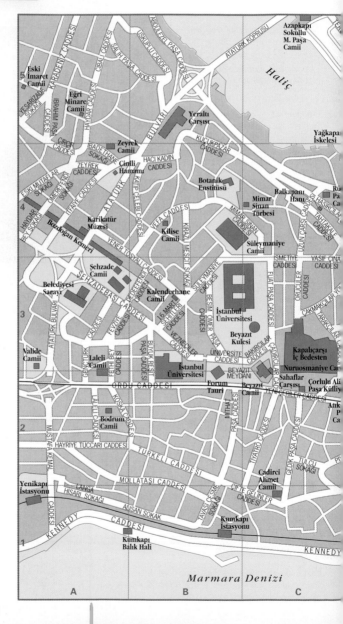

CENTRAL İSTANBUL EMİNÖNÜ

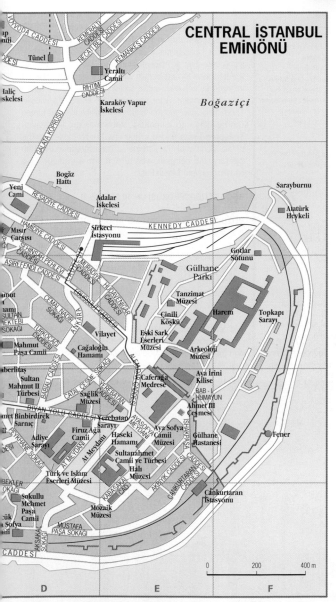

Boğaziçi

VOYVODA CADDESI

ap mii

Tünel

Yeraltı Camii

KEMERALTI CADDESI

NECATIBEY CADDESI

KEMANKEŞ CADDESI

Halic skelesi

RIHTIM CADDESI

Karaköy Vapur İskelesi

GALATA KÖPRÜSÜ

Yeni Cami

Boğaz Hattı

REŞADİYE CADDESI

Adalar İskelesi

Sarayburnu

Atatürk Heykeli

HAMIDIYE CADDESI

Mısır Çarşısı

ŞEHİNŞAH PEHLEVI

AŞIREFENDİ CADDESI

Sirkeci İstasyonu

KENNEDY CADDESI

MURADIYE CADDESI

EBÜSSUUD CADDESI

HÜDAVENDIGAR CADDESI

Gotlar Sütunu

Gülhane Parkı

ANKARA

CEMAL NADIR SOKAGI

TURKOCAGI

amut t amı SULTAN MEKTEBI SOKAGI

Tanzimat Müzesi

Çinili Köşkü

Harem

Topkapı Sarayı

Vilayet

Cağaloğlu Hamamı

Eski Şark Eserleri Müzesi

ALEMDAR CADDESI

Arkeoloji Müzesi

Mahmut Paşa Camii

berlitaş

Sultan Mahmut II Türbesi

BABIALI CADDESI

ÇATAL ÇEŞME SOKAGI

YEREBATAN CADDESI

Sağlik Müzesi

Caferağa Medrese

Aya İrini Kilise

BAB-I HÜMAYUN

Ahmet III Çeşmesi

DIVAN YOLU CADDESI

met Binbirdirek Sarnıç

FEYKHANE SOKAGI

Adiye Sarayı

Yerebatan Sarayı

Firuz Ağa Camii

AYASOFYA MEYDANI

At Meydanı

AT MEYDANI

Haseki Hamamı

Aya Sofya Camii Müzesi

İSHAKPAŞA CADDESI

Gülhane Hastanesi

Fener

Sultanahmet Camii ve Türbesi Halı Müzesi

Türk ve İslam Eserleri Müzesi

KABASAKAL CADI

AKBIYIK CADDESI

CANKURTARAN CADDESI

BEKLER OKAGI

Sokullu Mehmet Paşa Camii

Cankurtaran İstasyonu

ük Sofya ii

AKSAKAL SOKAGI

Mozaik Müzesi

MUSTAFA PAŞA SOKAGI

CADDESI

0   200   400 m

D   E   F

+ 38A2

✉ Mesih Paşa Caddesi, off
   Laleli Caddesi,
   Aksaray/Beyazıt

🕐 Crypt and cistern closed
   during prayer times, but
   can be viewed from stairs
   to right of minaret

🚋 Tram stop Laleli

♿ None

🎟 Free

↔ Beyazıt Meydanı (➤ 35),
   Laleli Camii (➤ 57)

BODRUM CAMİİ ✪

At the beginning of the 10th century, co-Emperor Romanus I Lecapenus built a church adjoining his palace, siting both over a 5th-century cistern. The church follows the traditional Byzantine plan with a narthex, a nave divided in three by columns and a small window-pierced dome over the transept. After his death, the emperor's widow, Theophano, gave up the luxuries of palace life and turned the building into a nunnery, known as the Myrelaion. Theophano was buried in the crypt, now closed to the public. Soon after the Ottoman conquest, late in the 15th century, the complex was turned into a mosque by a Muslim convert, Mesih Paşa.

BOĞAZİÇİ (BOSPHORUS) (➤ 19 AND 82–3)

+ 38A4

✉ Saraçhanebaşı Meydanı,
   between Fatih and
   Unkapanı

♿ Few

🎟 Free

↔ Fatih Camii (➤ 48),
   Kalenderhane Camii
   (➤ 53), Karikatür Müzesi
   (➤ 54), Şehzade Camii
   (➤ 66–7)

Valens' Aqueduct gives a Roman aspect to the city

BOZDOĞAN KEMERİ (VALENS' AQUEDUCT) ✪✪

It is impossible to ignore the city's past. Towering 186m above Atatürk Bulvarı, one of Istanbul's busiest boulevards, are the arches of an aqueduct built by Emperor Valens at the end of the 4th century. Originally 10km long, it brought clean water from the Belgrade Forest (➤ 84) to several cisterns around the city centre. The aqueduct was demolished by Heraclius in the 7th century, restored by Süleyman the Magnificent and used until the end of the 19th century to supply the city with water. More than 6km of impressive arches remain, connecting Istanbul's third and fourth hill. At the time of writing the arches are under restoration; there are plans for a promenade along the top.

The men's entrance to the 300-year-old Cağaloğlu Hamamı, with opening times and prices

BULGAR KİLİSE (CHURCH OF ST STEPHEN OF THE BULGARS) ⭐

Prefabricated in Vienna and constructed entirely of cast iron, this unusual 19th-century church was shipped down the Danube to be erected here in celebration of the moment in 1871 when the Bulgarian Orthodox Church declared independence from the Greek patriarch of Constantinople. The first Bulgarian patriarchs were buried here. Istanbul's small Bulgarian community continues to worship in this heavy-looking, cake-like church that appears somewhat lost in the middle of the Golden Horn road.

CAFERAĞA MEDRESE ⭐

This Koran school was built as a religious college in 1559 by Mimar Sinan for Caferağa, the chief black eunuch under Süleyman the Magnificent. A bust of the master architect graces the courtyard. The small cells where students once learned the Koran are now used as workshops by artisans who demonstrate such traditional skills as paper marbling, embroidery and ceramics. In summer the café is a good place to linger after visiting Aya Sofya.

CAĞALOĞLU HAMAMI ⭐⭐⭐

The famous and beautiful Cağaloğlu Hamamı were built in 1741 to pay for the upkeep of Mahmut I's library in nearby Aya Sofya (▶ 18). This is as close as you can get to having an Ottoman *hamam*, which is why you'll pay more to get in. A ring of columns supports the central dome of the cruciform steam room or *hararet*. Note the baroque marble basins and elaborate period taps.

✚ 28B4
✉ Mürsel Paşa Caddesi, Fener
🕐 Often locked, but guardian (usually in the garden) will open it for a small tip
🚢 Fener İskelesi (ferry landing)
♿ Few
🎟 Free, tip for guardian
🔁 Haghios Georgios (▶ 51)

✚ 39E2
✉ Caferiye Sokağı by Aya Sofya, Sultanahmet
🕐 Mon–Sat all day
🍴 Café (£) in the courtyard
🚋 Tram stop Sultanahmet
♿ Few
🎟 Free
🔁 Aya Sofya (▶ 18)

✚ 39D3
✉ 34 Yerebatan Caddesi, Sultanahmet. Women's entrance on Cağaloğlu Hamamı Sokak
🕐 Mon–Sat. Women 8–8; Men 7AM–10PM
🎟 Expensive for a *hamam*

41

To the Haliç (Golden Horn)

Distance
2.5km

Time
2–3 hours

Start point
⊞ 38A4
🚫 No public transport

End point
⊞ 38B5
⛴ Ferry stop Cibali İskelesi

Lunch
Cafeterias on the Golden Horn riverbank

Fine views across the Haliç towards Istanbul's Third Hill, capped by the Suleymaniye Camii

Take a taxi to Valens' Aqueduct (Bozdoğan Kemeri ➤ 40), which at its highest point crosses Atatürk Bulvarı. For a good view climb the stairs on either side of the avenue, but be very careful as there is no parapet. Housed in the 16th-century *medrese* near the aqueduct is the Karikatür Müzesi (➤ 54), which gives an interesting and valuable insight into Turkey's special brand of humour.

Walk right along the aqueduct to İtfaiye Caddesi.

After 200m, to the right you pass one of the most beautiful *hamamı* in the city, the Çinili Hamamı (Tiled Baths), designed by the master architect Sinan in 1545. This well-restored double *hamam* was built for the famous pirate Barbarossa.

Continue downhill and after 100m turn left to Zeyrek Camii (➤ 78).
After visiting the mosque, continue along İbadethane Sokak.

Zeyrek, a neighbourhood of steep streets, run-down wooden houses and small mosques, is picturesque and fascinating to stroll around.

Walk as far as Çırçır Caddesi and turn right on to Hacı Hasan Sokak, at the end of which is Eğri Minare Camii, the Mosque of the Crooked Minaret. Turn right and then immediately left to find Eski İmaret Camii.

This lovely 12th-century Byzantine church has one of the most striking exteriors of all Istanbul churches. The 12-sided dome is still tiled and the unusual designs in the brickwork include swastikas and Greek keys. (⊞ Only at prayer times.) Outside, on the square, take a minute to admire the fine views of the Haliç before continuing straight ahead, along Cibali Caddesi, to the attractive landscaped parkland along the western side of the Golden Horn.

ÇEMBERLİTAŞ (COLUMN OF CONSTANTINE) ★★

This blackened heap of stones supported by iron hoops may be a symbol of the city's endurance, but you would be forgiven for not noticing it at first. The column was erected by Constantine the Great on 11 May AD 330 to commemorate the dedication of Constantinople as the new capital of the Roman Empire. Made of Egyptian porphyry, the most precious of marbles at the time, it was originally topped with the gilded statue of the emperor and stood in the Forum of Constantine. In 1779 the column was burned in the same fire that destroyed the Covered Bazaar.

✚ 39D2
✉ Divan Yolu Caddesi
🚃 Tram stop Sultanahmet
♿ Good
🖐 Free
↔ Kapalıçarşı (➤ 20), Çorlulu Ali Paşa Külliyesi (➤ 43), Divan Yolu (➤ 44), Nuruosmaniye Camii (➤ 62)

For Turkish men and women the hamam is the perfect place to socialise and gossip

ÇEMBERLİTAŞ HAMAMI ★★

Built in 1584 by the powerful Valide Sultan Nur Banu, this *hamam* has long since lost its original decoration and its separate women's baths. It is conveniently close to the Kapalıçarşı (Covered Bazaar), and tourists are welcomed. Masseurs, used to handling uninitiated flesh, are not as heavy-handed as they are elsewhere, and it is therefore recommended for those trying a Turkish bath for the first time. The large, domed reception room is a wonderful place to relax afterwards.

✚ 39D2
✉ Vezirhanı Caddesi 8
☎ 522 79 74
🕐 9AM–7PM
🍴 Drinks (£)
🚃 Tram stop Çemberlitaş
♿ Few
🖐 Moderate for a *hamam*
↔ Kapalıçarşı (➤ 20) Nuruosmaniye (➤ 62)

ÇORLULU ALİ PAŞA KÜLLİYESİ ★★

A sign for 'the magical garden' leads to the *külliye* or pious foundation, built early in the 18th century by Ali Paşa. He was later exiled and executed, after which his severed head was placed in his tomb. Two carpet shops have now taken over the premises, one of which runs a charming tea house amongst the turbaned tombs in the garden. Sit here and drink *adaçayı* (sage tea) to soften the throat after smoking a *nargile*, or water pipe with honey-sweetened tobacco, and magic may well be in the air.

✚ 38C3
✉ Yeniçeriler Caddesi 36, Eminönü
🕐 Garden: until midnight. Closed Sun
🍴 Café (£)
🚃 Tram stop Sultanahmet
🖐 Free
↔ Kapalıçarşı (➤ 20), Atık Ali Paşa Camii (➤ 33)

29F5

✉ Dolmabahçe Caddesi
119, Beşiktaş

☎ 261 01 30

⏰ Wed–Sun 9:30–12:30,
1:30–5. Closed Mon, Tue

🚢 Beşiktaş Vapur İskelesi
(ferry landing)

♿ None

💷 Cheap

↔ Dolmabahçe Sarayı
(► 45), Yıldız Parkı
(► 78)

39D2

✉ Sultanahmet

🍴 Several restaurants (£ &
££), including the famous
Pudding Shop (£) (► 94)

🚋 Tram stop Sultanahmet

♿ Good

↔ Kapalıçarşı (► 20),
Yerebatan Sarayı (► 26),
Çemberlitaş (► 43),
Çorlulu Ali Paşa Külliyesi
(► 43), Nuruosmaniye
Camii (► 62)

---

*Dolmabahçe Sarayı
dominates the European
shore of the lower
Bosphorus*

DENİZ MÜZESİ (MARITIME MUSEUM)

The haphazard display of cannons and torpedoes in the garden isn't enticing, but the Maritime Museum does in fact house a fascinating collection of naval memorabilia. The first rooms are devoted to Atatürk and include the cabin from his yacht, *Savarona*. Elsewhere find a collection of miniature Ottoman soldiers, old maps (including a 16th-century chart of the North American coast), impressive swords and an assortment of Ottoman uniforms. Several displays are devoted to the notorious pirate-turned-Ottoman-admiral Hayrettin Paşa, known as Barbarossa. The highlight of the collection are the wonderful elegant wooden caiques used for rowing sultans between their palaces on the Bosphorus.

DİVAN EDEBİYATI MÜZESİ (DİVAN LITERATURE MUSEUM) SEE MEVLEVİ TEKKE (► 58)

DİVAN YOLU CADDESİ

Sooner or later a walk on Divan Yolu, the large avenue first laid out in Roman times, becomes inevitable. In Byzantine times this was the Mese, the Middle Way, and principal street. For the Ottomans, it was the main approach to the Divan, where the court could be petitioned. The small mound of stones in the square near Yerebatan Sarayı (► 26) was the navel of the Ottoman Empire, from where all distances in the empire were calculated. Near by, behind a railing, are several important tombs, including the domed *türbe* (mausoleum) of Sultan Mahmut II (► 69). In a garden to the left is the rare manuscript library of Köprülü. The Vezir Hani and the Çemberlitaş Hamamı (► 43), next to the Column of Constantine (► 43), were built by the same Köprülü family. Beyond the column the road changes name, to Yeniçeriler Caddesi (Avenue of the Janissaries) and then to Ordu Caddesi.

DOLMABAHÇE SARAYI ✪✪

Dolmabahçe is built on land recovered from the Bosphorus for the pleasure garden of a 17th-century sultan. The current *sarayı*, or palace, was completed in 1856 and consists of three parts, as was traditional: the *selamlık*, for men; the harem for the sultan and his extended family; and the state hall for official occasions. The palace – which was inhabited from 1855, when Sultan Abdülmecid moved the court here from the Topkapı Sarayı (➤ 24–5), until the end of the Ottoman Empire in 1922 – is often regarded as an insult to good taste, but a visit is essential for an insight into the last Ottoman years.

Any description of Dolmabahçe must fall back on figures: the overwhelming neo-classical white marble façade is 248m long, while the palace occupies 600m of waterfront. The state hall (2,000sq m) has the world's largest chandelier (4.5 tonnes of Bohemian glass, 750 lights). The central staircase has Baccarat crystal balusters. The corridors, which could accommodate a parade of elephants, link over 280 rooms, 43 salons and 6 *hamamı*.

The harem occupies some two-thirds of the palace. Amidst a succession of rooms for the sultan's mother, favourite and official wives, and concubines, there is the small room in which Atatürk died at 09:05 on 10 November 1938. Antique clocks on display in museums throughout Turkey stand still at that time in his honour.

🕇 29F4
✉ Dolmabahçe Caddesi, Beşiktaş
☎ 258 55 44
🕘 9–4. Closed Mon, Thu. Guided tours only
🍴 Tea rooms (£) with snacks
🚌 Bus 210 or 56 from Sultanahmet; many from Taksim, Eminönü and Beşiktaş
🚢 Beşiktaş İskelesi (ferry landing)
♿ None
💷 Very expensive; separate tickets for harem and *selamlık*
↔ Deniz Müzesi (➤ 44)
❓ Avoid Sunday, as it gets very crowded. Reserve tickets in advance by phone

Above: *Dolmabahçe's central stairway, framed with columns of marble*

45

In the Know

If you only have a short time to visit Istanbul, or would like to get a real flavour of the city, here are some ideas:

Watch out when buying a carpet and shop around first to get an idea of quality and prices

10
Ways to Be a Local

Learn as many words and basic phrases in Turkish as you can. Istanbulis always appreciate being greeted respectfully.

Take off your shoes before entering a mosque or a shrine. Dress modestly, covering up legs and arms. Women should cover their heads.

Bargain hard, but get an idea of the price first and avoid guides, however friendly.

Eat *alaturka*, the Turkish way, and when invited taste every dish served but never take twice. Never blow your nose at the table.

Get a breath of fresh air and have a picnic in Yıldız Parkı (➤ 78).

In summer move to the Adalar, or Princes' Islands (➤ 84) together with thousands of Istanbuli families, escaping the city's heat and pollution for a car-free zone.

Have a Turkish breakfast (*kahvaltı*): starting with *çorba* (soup), *börek* filled with mince or cheese, or a *simit*, bread ring with sesame seeds, all sold on street stalls.

Joke like a Turk, but first visit the Karikatür Müzesi (➤ 54) to get an insight into Turkish humour.

Look for junk or second-hand books in the Sunday Market in Ortaköy (➤ 63) or hang out in one of the trendy bars.

Spend the night in a wooden house in old Istanbul: Yeşil Ev (➤ 101), Aya sofya Pansiyonları (➤ 100), Kariye (➤ 100), Empress Zoe (➤ 100).

10
Good Places to Have Lunch

Pandeli (££) (➤ 94) Good traditional Turkish dishes and a wonderful view over the Mısır Çarşısı.

Kumkapı (££) ✉ İstasyon Caddesi 21 ☎ 517 22 54 Many excellent fish restaurants, including Kartallar.

Hacı Abdullah (£) (➤ 92) For kebabs and preserved fruits.

Hala (£) (➤ 93) Home of Anatolian speciality ravioli in yoghurt sauce.

Pizzeria Gold (£) İstiklâl Caddesi, near Çiçek Passage ☎ 293 84 51 Excellent pizzas.

Deniz (£–££) (➤ 98) One of the best fish restaurants on the European shore.

Konyalı Topkapı (££) (➤ 93) An imperial view of the Bosphorus and the Sea of Marmara, accompanied by great food.

Darüzziyafe (££) (➤ 92) Delicious Turkish food served beneath a stunning vault, next to Süleymaniye Camii.

Havuzlu (£) (➤ 93) The best in the bazaar.

Kanaat Lokantası (£) (➤ 93) Has been serving excellent Turkish food since 1933.

10
Top Activities

Take a boat and avoid the traffic jams.

Smoke like a Turk: water pipes in Piyer Loti Café (➤ 97) and the café in Çorlulu Ali Paşa Külliyesi (➤ 43).

Have a good scrub at Çemberlitaş (➤ 43) or Galatasaray Hamamı ✉ Turnacıbaşı Sokak 2, off İstiklâl Caddesi.

Watch the Whirling Dervishes at Mevlevi Tekke (Divan Edebiyatı Müzesi) (➤ 58) ☎ 245-41 41.

Visit a yalı on the Bosphorus: the Sadberk Hanım Müzesi (➤ 66).

Buy a carpet in the Arasta Bazaar (➤ 51) or in Roxelana Hamamı (➤ 64).

Get lost in the Kapalıçarşı (Covered Bazaar), and wander off the beaten track (➤ 20).

Have a sugar overdose eating Turkish delights at Hacı Bekir (➤ 97) or try home-made jams at Üç Yıldız (➤ 109).

Go back in time and have tea in the grand tea room of the Pera Palas Oteli (➤ 63).

Walk along the Bosphorus and eat fish near Rumeli Hisarı, Sarıyer or Büyükdere.

Many Istanbulis pick up a simit or ring of sesame bread for breakfast

5
Best Viewpoints

Galata Tower (➤ 50) for a 14th-century view on Istanbul.

Seraglio Point in Gülhane Parkı (➤ 51), once the preserve of the Sultan.

Piyer Loti Café, Eyüp (➤ 97), in a romantic mood.

Rooftop of Büyük Valide Hanı, an old caravanserai between the Spice Bazaar and the Covered Bazaar.

Üsküdar (➤ 74–5) for a skyline of domes and minarets.

5
Best Places for Street Food

Fish Market, İstiklâl Caddesi (➤ 53). Cheap but delicious sandwiches with fried sardines or mussels.

Sultanahmet Selim Usta, Divan Yolu Caddesi 12a. Some of the area's best meat balls and kebabs.

İstiklâl Caddesi (➤ 53) serving really excellent kebabs.

Around the Spice Bazaar (Mısır Çarşısı) (➤ 59). Good dried fruit snacks.

Near the Galata Bridge in Eminönü, where fishermen sell their catch grilled.

10
Best Mosques

Rüstem Paşa Camii (➤ 65), by Sinan, for its tiles and bird's-eye view of the Covered Bazaar.

Sultan Selim Camii (➤ 69) for its position, overlooking the Haliç.

Şehzade Camii (➤ 66–7) for its splendour (Sinan).

Sokullu Mehmet Paşa Camii (➤ 68) for the excellent İznik tiles and the calligraphy lost in tulips.

Sultanahmet Camii for grandeur (➤ 23).

Süleymaniye Camii (➤ 22), designed by Sinan, simply the city's finest.

Beyazıt Camii (➤ 34) for being the oldest great mosque in town.

Eyüp Sultan Camii (➤ 48), one of Islam's most holy places.

Hırka-i Şerif Camii (➤ 52) for its unusual minarets.

Şemsi Paşa Camii (➤ 75) for being small and pretty (Sinan).

🚩 29E4
✉ Sarayarkası Sokak
   33–35, Gümüşsuyu
🕐 Tue–Sat 8:30–7.
⛴ Kabataş Vapur İskelesi

🚩 28A5
✉ West bank of the Haliç
🕐 Mosque: during prayer
   times. Café: daily
🍴 Piyer Loti café (£)
🚌 Bus 33 or 99 from
   Eminönü
🚢 Boat from Eminönü or
   Karaköy to Ayvansaray,
   and then short walk
♿ None
💲 Free
↔ Haliç (▶ 52)

🚩 28B3
✉ Tophane Sokağı, off
   İslambol Caddesi, Fatih
🕐 Tomb 9:30–4:30. Closed
   Mon
🚌 Bus 91 from Eminönü
♿ None
💲 Free
↔ Hırka-i Şerif Camii
   (▶ 52), Kız Taşı (▶ 55),
   Mesih Mehmet Paşa
   Camii (▶ 57)

ERCÜMENT KALMİK MÜZESİ   😊

The work of one of Turkey's best-known modern artists, Ercüment Kalmik, is displayed in a museum and arts centre in a lovely old house. The arts centre also organises exhibitions of work by other contemporary artists.

EYÜP SULTAN CAMİİ   😊😊

Eyüp Ensari, friend and standard bearer of the Prophet Muhammad, is believed to have been killed here during the Arab siege of Constantinople in AD 670. Turks consider his tomb the most sacred place in the Islamic world after Mecca and Jerusalem. It is beautifully decorated with magnificent İznik tiles. The present mosque, approached through a particularly delightful shaded courtyard, was built in the 19th century after earthquakes destroyed its predecessors. Go up through the peaceful cemetery to the café, where the young French naval officer Pierre Loti (1850–1923) wrote of his tragic love for a harem girl, Aziyade. The café enjoys great views over the Haliç.

FATİH CAMİİ (MOSQUE OF SULTAN MEHMET   😊😊
THE CONQUEROR)

The imperial mosque of Mehmet II, with its large dome and slender minarets, crowns Istanbul's Fourth Hill and can be seen from all over the city. The largest mosque of the Ottoman Empire, it was built in the 15th century on the site of Constantine's Church of the Holy Apostles, where for hundreds of years Byzantine emperors had been buried. The mosque's Greek architect was put to death when the sultan discovered that his dome was lower than that of the Aya Sofya. The mosque was rebuilt after an earthquake in 1766. The courtyard, with a lovely central

The spacious interior of
Eyüp Sultan Camii

ablution fountain, belongs to the original 15th-century
building. Note the early İznik tiles around the windows on
the west wall. The marble mausoleum of Mehmet II and
the tomb of his wife Gülbahar are in the garden behind the
mosque. In the morning the terrace around the mosque
becomes an extension of the nearby market and is a
wonderful place to watch the world go by.

FENARİ İSA CAMİİ

The intriguing monastic Church of Theotokos Panachrantos
(the Immaculate Mother of God) was originally built by the
10th-century courtier Constantine Lips. In the 13th century
the Empress Theodora added another church, which
explains its unusual seven apses along the eastern façade.
In 1496 the church was converted to a mosque by a Sufi
community who named it Fenari İsa or the 'Lamp of
Jesus'. The interior reveals well-restored barrel vaulting
and intricate brickwork with unusual designs. On the roof
there are several small chapels around the southern dome.

FETHİYE CAMİİ (CHURCH OF THEOTOKOS
PAMMAKARISTOS)

The 12th-century Church of the Joyous Mother of God was
one of the few churches to survive the Muslim conquest
intact and served as the patriarchate of Constantinople until
1568. Some years later it was converted into a mosque.
While the central chamber still serves as a mosque, the
parekklesion (side chapel) is now a museum conserving
exquisite and emotive late Byzantine mosaics that show
Christ Pantocrator and Apostles, Christ Hyperagathos, the
Virgin and St John the Baptist (entry by special permission
from the Directorate at Aya Sofya).

✚ 28B2
✉ North side of Adnan
Menderes (Vatan)
Caddesi, Fatih
🕐 Praying hours
♿ None
💷 Free
↔ Fatih Camii (➤ 48), Kız
Taşı (➤ 55), Murat Paşa
Camii (➤ 62)

✚ 28B4
✉ Fethiye Kapısı Sokak,
Fatih
🕐 Hours of prayer. Chapel
usually closed
🚌 Bus 91 from Eminönü or
86 from Taksim Square
♿ None
💷 Free
↔ Kariye Camii (➤ 21),
Nişancı Mehmet Paşa
Camii (➤ 62)

From Galata Bridge watch streams of people walk along the waterfront

✚ 29D3
✉ Over the Haliç between Eminönü and Galata
🍴 Under the bridge food stalls sell fresh sardines
🛳 Eminönü or Karaköy ferry landing
♿ Good
↔ Galata Kulesi (➤ 50), Mısır Çarşısı (➤ 59)

GALATA KÖPRÜSÜ (GALATA BRIDGE) ✪✪✪

Officially called Karaköy Köprüsü, but still known under its old name, the bridge over the Haliç (Golden Horn) between Galata and Eminönü is one of the most lively places in Istanbul. Its proximity to bazaars, ferry landings and big banks ensures a constant flow of people and cars. Anglers cast off at all hours of the day. The first bridge on this site was a wooden one, built in 1845. The fourth was home to popular but rough restaurants and cafés. The owners reportedly set fire to it as the present bridge, the fifth one – a six-lane highway – loomed above them.

✚ 29D3
✉ Galip Dede Caddesi, Şişhane
☎ 245 11 60
🕐 Daily 9–8. Nightclub after 8PM
🍴 Restaurant (££) and nightclub with oriental show
♿ Few
💰 Moderate
↔ Galata Köprüsü (➤ 50), İstiklâl Caddesi (➤ 53), Mevlevi Tekke (➤ 58)

GALATA KULESİ (GALATA TOWER) ✪✪

The Galata Tower, 61m high and 140m above sea level, happens to offer wonderful views, but it was built in 1348 as a bastion to reinforce Genoese defences. During the Ottoman era, the tower served as an observatory and invaluable fire look-out. In 1960 it became a tourist attraction and a lift was installed to the penultimate floor, where stairs lead to a restaurant-nightclub and an observation deck. On a clear day you can see over the Bosphorus, Golden Horn, Galata and Eminönü. At the top, read the story of Hefarzen Ahmet Çelebi, who in the 17th century, equipped with wings he himself designed, flew over the Bosphorus from the tower, landing safely in Üsküdar on the Asian shore.

Right: the Genoese Galata Tower

GÜLHANE PARKI

Occupants of the Topkapı Sarayı were lucky enough to enjoy superb views of the Bosphorus from their gardens. The Rose Garden (Gül Hane) on the lower terrace has now been turned into a wooded public park, making this blessed corner of the city accessible to all. The central promenade leads past kiosks, a café and a rather depressing little zoo, with skinny dogs, cats and even chickens in cages. Unexpectedly, at the end of the park you come to one of the city's oldest monuments, the Goth's Column, a 3rd-century AD granite column capped with a Corinthian capital. Its Latin inscription reads: 'To the prosperity that returned with the defeat of the Goths'. From the nearby sultan's private garden, now a popular picnic spot, there are excellent views of the Bosphorus. Further west towards Galata Bridge, near the 17th-century Basket-Weavers' Kiosk, is another garden and a good waterfront bar.

HAGHİOS GEORGİOS (CHURCH OF ST GEORGE)

St George's Church has been the seat of the Greek Orthodox Patriarch of Constantinople since 1601. Entirely rebuilt in 1720, it is a simple basilica (domes were at that time banned for churches) with an impressive wooden iconostasis. Note the exceptionally fine pair of mosaics of the Virgin with Child and St John the Baptist. The church houses several treasures, including the patriarchal throne, inlaid with mother-of-pearl, and the reliquaries of three saints.

HALI MÜZESİ

This is a wonderful collection of mainly 16th- and 17th-century kilims and carpets, well displayed against a plain marble background. At the time of writing the kilim section was closed for restoration. If this gives you the urge to buy your own rug, visit the Arasta Bazaar in the old stables next door, home to some of the city's better carpet shops.

Visit the rich collection of rugs and kilims at the Halı Müzesi before venturing into a nearby carpet shop

51

Another day, another sunset on the Golden Horn, which in this light regains its old magic

HALİÇ (GOLDEN HORN)   ●●●

According to legend the Golden Horn was so called because during the Ottoman siege of the city the Byzantine population threw all their valuable possessions into its waters. The Golden Horn is one of the finest natural harbours in the world and its name may also have reflected the wealth it brought the city. Once its banks were the magnificent pleasure gardens of sultans and great Ottoman families, but in time these made way for factories, apartment blocks and workshops, and the waters became so polluted they began to reek. Now, a rehabilitation programme to restore the Golden Horn to something of its former glory has begun, and stretches of its banks are again being turned into public gardens. There is still some way to go, however, before rulers would choose to linger here.

HASEKİ HAMAMI SEE ROXELANA HAMAMI (➤ 64)

HIPPODROME (AT MEYDANI) (➤ 17, TOP TEN)

HIRKA-İ ŞERİF CAMİİ   ●●

The small sanctuary behind the *mihrab* of this Mosque of the Holy Mantle houses the Prophet Muhammad's cloak. Built in 1851 by Sultan Abdülmecid I, the mosque has an elegant neo-Renaissance façade with unusually large windows and a pair of minarets shaped like Corinthian columns. The sumptuous octagonal prayer hall, constantly busy with pilgrims, is decorated with a splendid entablature and a fine calligraphic frieze.

Sidebar (left column, upper):

✚ 28C4
🚢 Ferries from Eminönü to several stations along the Haliç
♿ Few
💶 Free
↔ Bulgar Kilise (➤ 41), Eyüp Sultan Camii (➤ 48), Galata Köprüsü (➤ 50), Haghios Georgios (➤ 51), Mısır Çarşısı (➤ 59)

Sidebar (left column, lower):

✚ 28B3
✉ Keçeciler Caddesi, Fatih
🕐 Hours of prayer
♿ None
💶 Free
↔ Mesih Mehmet Paşa Camii (➤ 57), Nişancı Mehmet Paşa Camii (➤ 62)

İMRAHOR CAMİİ (CHURCH OF ST JOHN THE BAPTIST OF STUDIUS) ★★

Istanbul's oldest church, built in AD 463 and now one of its finest ruins, was named after its patron, the Consul Studius. For 1,000 years it was one of Constantinople's spiritual and intellectual centres, but in the 15th century it was turned into a mosque by an İmrahor (Equerry) of Sultan Beyazıt II. In 1894 it was half-ruined by an earthquake and was abandoned. Four Corinthian capitals and the architrave of the entrance are beautifully carved and the floor is paved in colourful marble mosaics. The family that squats on the grounds now makes a small income from tips.

🔳 28A1
✉ İmam Aşir Sokağı, off İmrahor İlyas Caddesi, İmrahor
🕐 Open daily
🚆 Train station Yedikule (from Sirkeci)
🚫 None
💷 Free, tip for the family that guards the church
🔁 Theodosian Walls (➤ 71), Yedikule (➤ 76)

İSTİKLÂL CADDESİ ★★★

The pedestrian heart of Beyoğlu is the former Grande Rue de Pera, lined with some of the city's better shops, galleries and old embassy buildings (Walk ➤ 77). The French Embassy was the oldest, built in 1581 and rebuilt after a fire in 1831. The embassies became consulates when the capital moved to Ankara. Further down is the Çiçek Pasajı and its many restaurants, and the Balık Pazarı (Fish Market), a colourful food market. On the next square the elite Galatasaray School stands behind a massive gateway. Once notorious for its sleazy nightlife, the area has been cleaned up but has retained a certain amount of atmosphere and appeal. Some of the bars and restaurants are still worth checking out. The old-fashioned tramway from Tünel to Taksim Square adds to the street's retro feel.

🔳 29D4
✉ Beyoğlu
🕐 Daily morning–evening; many shops even open on Sunday
🍴 Many restaurants (£–££) see Restaurant section
🚇 Tünel
🚫 Few
💷 Free
🔁 Galata Kulesi (➤ 50), Mevlevi Tekke (➤ 58), Taksim Meydanı (➤ 70)

Trams add to the atmosphere of İstiklâl Caddesi

KALENDERHANE CAMİİ (CHURCH OF THEOTOKOS KYRIOTISSA) ★★

The 9th-century Church of Our Lady, Mother of God, is one of the most beautiful Byzantine buildings to have survived in Istanbul. The church was converted into a mosque shortly after the Ottoman conquest in the 15th century and assigned to the Kalender Sufi brotherhood. Much of the original marble decoration is retained, while a series of fine 13th-century frescoes on the life of Francis of Assisi, uncovered during renovation work in 1953, is now in the Archaeological Museum (➤ 16).

🔳 38B3
✉ 16 Mart Sehitleri Caddesi, Beyazıt
🕐 Hours of prayer
🚫 None
💷 Free
🔁 Süleymaniye Camii (➤ 22), Beyazıt Meydanı (➤ 35), Bozdoğan Kemeri (➤ 40), Şehzade Camii (➤ 66)

The courtyard of Istanbul's Caricature Museum

KAPALIÇARŞI (COVERED BAZAAR) (▶ 20, TOP TEN)

KARA AHMED PAŞA CAMİİ ✪

Ahmet Paşa was a Grand Vizier of Süleyman the Magnificent, and the imperial architect Sinan built this small mosque for him in 1554. An attractive tree-shaded courtyard is surrounded by a colonnade; off it is the *medrese* (Islamic school). The perfectly proportioned building exudes a wonderful sense of harmony. Panels above the prayer-hall windows are decorated with blue and green İznik tiles that are unusual for their Arabesque designs.

🔢 28A3
📩 Topkapı Caddesi, near Topkapı Gate in the Theodosian Walls
🕐 Hours of prayer
🚊 Tram from Sirkeci or Sultanahmet to Topkapı
♿ None
🖐 Free
↔ Theodosian Walls (▶ 71)

KARİKATÜR MÜZESİ ✪
(CARICATURE MUSEUM)

Turks love a joke and political cartoons have become an essential part of the daily papers. The Caricature Museum, housed in a 16th-century *medrese* with a lovely garden, near the Bozdoğan Kemeri (Valens' Aqueduct), has a display of cartoons that changes each week – a good insight into Turkish humour. It runs several workshop classes including drawing and silk screen.

🔢 38A4
📩 Atatürk Bulvarı,
📞 521 12 64
🕐 Tue–Sun 10–5
♿ Few
🖐 Cheap
↔ Bozdoğan Kemeri (▶ 41), Şehzade Camii (▶ 66)

KARİYE CAMİİ (▶ 21, TOP TEN)

Did you know ?

After the Ottoman Conquest many churches were converted to mosques. Christians were subsequently not allowed to build churches with domes, so all the later churches, including the Haghios Georgios (▶ 51), were constructed as simple basilicas with wooden roofs.

KILIÇ ALİ PAŞA CAMİİ ✪

When the great Admiral Kılıç Ali Paşa asked Sultan Murat III where to build his mosque, the response was somehow obvious: 'Where admirals belong, in the sea'. Ali Paşa then filled in part of the Bosphorus shore and commissioned Sinan to build a mosque complex. Not for the first time, the architect took his inspiration from the plan of the Aya Sofya (➤ 18), but this is one of his lesser creations: the interior seems loaded and heavy, though the *mihrab* is decorated with İznik tiles from the finest period. Behind the mosque is the admiral's hexagonal tomb, a *medrese* and the black dome of the (still-functioning) *hamam* (Turkish bath).

The fountain of Tophane (Tophane Çeşmesi), near the mosque, was built by Sultan Mahmut I in 1732. Similar to the fountain in Üsküdar Square, the elegant rococo structure is decorated with reliefs of flowers and fruits. It was named after the nearby Tophane, or cannon foundry, which dates from just after the conquest by Mehmet II.

✚ 29D3
✉ Necatibey Caddesi, Tophane
🕐 Prayer hours
♿ None
💷 Free

Marcian's Column stands isolated in the centre of a roundabout

KIZ TAŞI (MARCIAN'S COLUMN) ✪

Kız Taşı, the Maiden's Column, now stands forlorn in the middle of a roundabout. A Roman column of Corinthian marble and granite, it probably supported a statue of the Emperor Marcian (450–7). The Latin text on the plinth states that it was erected in his honour.

✚ 28B2
✉ Kıztaşı Caddesi, Fatih
♿ Good
💷 Free
↔ Fatih, Camii (➤ 48),

KOCA MUSTAFA PAŞA CAMİİ ✪

Grand Vizier Koca Mustafa Paşa converted the Byzantine Church of St Andrew to a mosque at the beginning of the 16th century, adding the five-domed porch, a Dervish monastery, mausoleums and a *hamam*. Some original details of the church are still visible, including the dome with masterfully worked 6th-century capitals. Pilgrims flock to the tombs of the sheikhs in the garden, particularly that of the first sheikh Sümbül (Hyacinth) and his daughter Rahine, who were once regarded as the city's patron saints.

✚ 28A1
✉ Koca Mustafa Paşa Caddesi, Fatih
🕐 Prayer hours
♿ None
💷 Free
↔ Ramazan Efendi Camii (➤ 64), Theodosian Walls at Silivrikapı (➤ 71)

The exquisitely carved capitals and entablature of columns in the Küçük Ayasofya

🏛 39D1
✉ Mehmet Paşa Sokak, Cankurtaran/Kadırga
🕐 10:30–5:30
♿ None
💰 Free
↔ At Meydanı (➤ 17), Sultanahmet Camii (➤ 23), Sokullu Mehmet Paşa Camii (➤ 68)

KÜÇÜK AYASOFYA CAMİİ ★★
(SS SERGIUS AND BACCHUS CHURCH)

'The Little Mosque of Ayasofya', so called because it looks like a scale model of the great basilica, predates it by ten years (AD 527). It was dedicated by the Emperor Justinian to Sergius and Bacchus, the martyred patrons of Christians in the Roman army. Justinian had good reason to remember the saints: legend has it that his uncle and predecessor, Emperor Justin I, was planning to have Justinian executed, until the Christian saints appeared to Justin in a dream and pleaded for his nephew's life. For over 1,000 years, the beautiful church was one of the city's richest sanctuaries, until in the 16th century Hüseyin Ağa, chief black eunuch under Sultan Beyazıt II, converted it to a mosque. Hüseyin Ağa's tomb lies to the north of the apse.

The traditional brick exterior gives no hint of the odd beauty of the interior, an irregular octagon set in an irregular rectangle. Some pillars on the ground floor still bear Justinian's monogram and a beautifully carved frieze honours Justinian, his wife Theodora and Sergius. Bacchus, for some unknown reason, was left out. The main 16-faceted dome is supported by eight polygonal piers separated by pairs of magnificent red and green marble columns – a surprisingly colourful screen.

Far right: Mesih Mehmet Paşa Camii is encircled by some of Istanbul's main streets

🏛 82C3
✉ Asian shore of the lower Bosphorus
🕐 9–4. Closed Mon, Thu
🚢 Anadoluhisarı İskelesi (ferry landing) or bus from Çengelköy İskelesi
💰 Cheap
↔ Anadolu Hisarı (➤ 32)

KÜÇÜKSU KASRI ★★

Sultan Abdülmecid I's splendid rococo palace was intended to be an escape from the Dolmabahçe Sarayı (➤ 45). Built by the same architect and finished in 1857, it echoes the Dolmabahçe's emphasis on opulence. The façade is a riot of swags and plinths and frills, while the interior glitters with crystal chandeliers and gilded panels. The setting, on a meadow formed by the two rivers known as the 'Sweet Waters of Asia', remains magnificent.

LALELİ CAMİİ ⭐

Sultan Mustafa III's elegant Tulip Mosque is a perfect example of Ottoman baroque. It was built between 1759 and 1763 on a high terrace above a busy covered market. Like Kücük Ayasofya, the plan is an octagon, but here set in a perfect rectangle. All the walls are richly inlaid with marbles of yellow, red, blue and other colours – note the extravagant medallions of marbles, onyx, lapis and other semi-precious stones in the gallery along the west wall.

- 38A3
- Ordu Caddesi, Aksaray
- Prayer hours
- Tramway from Sirkeci, Sultanahmet
- None
- Free
- Beyazıt Meydanı (► 35), Bodrum Camii (► 40), Murat Paşa Camii (► 62)

MAHMUT PAŞA CAMİİ ⭐

This 15th-century mosque founded by Mahmut Paşa is one of the oldest in the city, but more notable is his enchanting mausoleum. It is decorated in what is for Istanbul an unusual Moorish style, with marble inlaid with zellig mosaics (coloured ceramic tiles). Near by, on Mahmut Paşa Hamam Sokağı, in Mahmut Paşa's *hamam*, the superb carved plaster is currently being restored.

- 39D3
- Vezirhanı Caddesi, Çemberlitaş
- Prayer hours
- None
- Free
- Kapalıçarşı (► 20)

MESİH MEHMET PAŞA CAMİİ ⭐⭐

Mesih Mehmet, a eunuch with a reputation for cruelty and a one-time governor of Egypt, built his mosque in 1585 on a high terrace overlooking a garden. Inside the mosque the lovely *mihrab* (prayer niche) is framed by finest-quality İznik tiles. The *mihrab*, *mimbar* and grilles over the windows are beautifully worked in marble. His tomb, in a *türbe* in the centre of the little courtyard, is much venerated by locals.

- 28B3
- Akşemsettin Caddesi, Fatih
- Prayer hours. Tomb: Tue–Sun 9:30–4:30.
- None
- Free
- Hırka-i Şerif Camii (► 52)

29D3
Galip Dede Caddesi 15, Tünel
245 41 41
Tue–Sun 9:30–5. Closed Mon
Tünel, or tramway from Taksim Meydanı
Few
Moderate
Galata Kulesi (► 50), İstiklâl Caddesi (► 53)
Performance of the 'Sema dance' and Sufi music last Sunday of every month

MEVLEVİ TEKKE (DİVAN LITERATURE MUSEUM) ✪✪

The *tekke* (monastery) of the Mevlevi brotherhood, also known as the Galata Mevlevihanesi or Whirling Dervishes, was the heart of Istanbul's musical and poetic life from its construction in 1491 until the 1920s, when Atatürk abolished the Sufi orders. The original building, much altered, remains something of a retreat in the city. The 18th-century octagonal lodge now houses the Divan Literature Museum (Divan Edebiyatı Müzesi), with a fine display of Sufi musical instruments, Dervish accessories and original illuminated manuscripts of Turkish court poetry. There are regular performances and concerts of Sufi music and dances. In the lovely overgrown garden cemetery, cats play around fallen tombstones. Galip Dede, who gave his name to the street, was a celebrated 17th-century Mevlevi poet.

29F3
Fevzi Paşa Caddesi, off Edirnekapı, Fatih
Hours of prayer
Bus 99 from Eminönü
None
Free
Kariye Camii (► 21), Tekfur Sarayı (► 70), Theodosian Walls (► 71)

MİHRİMAH CAMİİ ✪✪

Built in the 1560s by Süleyman the Magnificent for his favourite daughter, Mihrimah, this is one of the purest and most innovative mosques in Istanbul designed by the architect Sinan. Crowning the top of the Sixth Hill, the Mihrimah rises majestically above the land walls (► 71) and the Edirne Gate. The courtyard, with an ablution fountain at its centre, is enclosed by colonnades and the cells of the Koranic school. The mosque is entered through a porch of seven domed bays supported by granite and marble columns. The building deserves its nickname of the Mosque of Two Hundred Windows: its vast hall is magnificently lit by rows of stained-glass windows set around the base of the soaring central dome and, unusually, in the supporting walls. The plan of this mosque, the second that Sinan built for the princess, influenced many baroque and rococo structures around the city.

Stunning mosaics from a colonnaded walkway in the Great Palace of Emperor Constantine I

A feast for the senses at the Egyptian Bazaar, with herbs, Turkish delights and fragrant essential oils

MISIR ÇARŞISI (EGYPTIAN SPICE BAZAAR) ⭐⭐⭐

A small covered market, the Spice Bazaar is an empire of the senses, a great place to linger, to savour magic smells and find something delicious to take home. The bazaar was originally built in 1600 as a 'drugstore' attached to the Yeni Cami complex (► 76). Its association with Egypt was financial: the foundation received an income from tax levied in Egypt. Where Genoese and Venetian traders once sold spices, medicinal plants and perfumes, Turkish traders continue the tradition and in a handful of the 88 original vaulted shops you can follow in the footsteps of 19th-century travellers by sampling henna, sandalwood, cinnamon, pistachios and a host of other aromatic and herbal goods; opium and hashish are no longer on offer. Other shops sell apple tea, Iranian caviar, Turkish delights and other treats. Pandeli restaurant(► 94), over the market entrance, offers simple Turkish food and good market views. There are more excellent shops between here and the Kapalıçarşı (Covered Bazaar) (► 20).

🚩 39D4
✉️ Yeni Cami Caddesi, Eminönü
🕐 Mon–Sat 9–6. Closed Sun
🍴 Pandeli (££) (► 94)
🚌 All buses to Eminönü
⛴️ All boats to Eminönü
♿ Good
🎟️ Free
🔄 Kapalıçarşı (► 20), Galata Köprüsü (► 50), Yeni Cami (► 76)

MOZAİK MÜZESİ ⭐⭐

Constantine I's Great Palace occupied the south side of the Hippodrome (At Meydanı) (► 17) and remained the imperial residence for 900 years. All that survives is a 6th-century mosaic pavement, believed to have linked the imperial apartments with the Hippodrome. This is now displayed *in situ* along with other architectural fragments. Amongst the extraordinary mosaic images, look out for an elephant strangling a lion, an eagle fighting a snake and Dionysos with a fruity beard. The museum is opposite the Arasta Bazaar.

🚩 39E1
✉️ Torun Sokağı, Sultanahmet
☎️ 518 12 05
🕐 Wed–Mon 9:30–5
🚊 Tram stop Sultanahmet
♿ Few
🎟️ Moderate
🔄 Sultanahmet Camii (► 23), Halı Müzesi (► 51)

59

Food & Drink

Sweet Delights
Popular desserts include rice pudding, *ayva* or *kabak tatlısı* (baked quince or pumpkin with clotted cream and nuts), *gül reçeli* (rose petal preserve) and *aşure* (pudding with raisins, nuts, almonds, pine nuts, figs and pistachios). Pastries such as *baklava* (filo with pistachios marinated in honey) and *künefe* (angelhair stuffed with nuts or cream) and *lokums* are eaten any moment of the day. In summer Istanbulis go crazy for *dondurma*, home-made ice cream.

Top: *sweet delights*
Above right: *grilled fish along the waterfront*

The Turks were originally nomads and as such adapted their cuisine to their changing circumstances and to the different places in which they lived. Based on good fresh produce and respecting the natural taste of the ingredients, Turkish cuisine is healthy and varied. It also reflects the country's long history, clearly showing Greek, Iranian and Middle Eastern influences. Eating out in Istanbul is relatively cheap, and food is not necessarily better when it is more expensive: some of the more memorable culinary experiences may very well be serendipitous – the fresh sardine sandwich you picked up from the fishing boat under the Galata Bridge (➤ 47) or the fried mussel snack you bought in Galata Fish Market (➤ 47, 53). *Bon appetit*, or as the Turks say, *afiyet olsun*.

Meze (Appetisers)

Çorba (soup) and salads are usually on offer, but it can be more interesting to start a meal with a selection of *meze* (appetisers), which can be stretched to make a meal in themselves. *Meze* may also be the ideal meal for vegetarians since many dishes are made of freshly cooked vegetables and pulses. Traditional *meze* include delicious *börek* (filo pastry filled with cheese, spinach or meat), *yaprak dolma* (vine leaves stuffed with rice, spices and pine nuts), *biber dolma* or alternatively *lahana dolma* (stuffed peppers or cabbage), *imam bayıldı* (stuffed aubergine with onions, tomatoes and spices served cold), *zeytinyağli enginar* (artichoke hearts), *pastırma* (dried meat with fenugreek), *patlican salatası* (aubergine purée), *semizotu* (purslane) and *turşu* (pickled vegetables). The best way to eat *meze* is with bread and a glass of wine or *rakı*.

Above: *the great variety of Turkish meze offers something for everyone*

60

Meat

The main course is usually a meat dish. Vegetarians should be aware that what appear to be vegetable dishes such as beans, chickpeas or vegetable stews are often cooked in a meat broth. Most meat comes grilled as a variety of kebab such as *İskender kebab* (grilled lamb on flat bread and yoghurt), *Adana kebab* (spicy lamb with sumac spice), *döner* (sliced meat cooked on a spit) or *köfte* (meat balls). *Güveç* is a stew of peppers, aubergines, tomatoes and lamb cubes, and *saç kavurma* is a wok-fried dish of meat, vegetables and spices.

Offal is popular, especially *böbrek* (kidney), *yürek* (heart), *ciğer* (liver) and *koç yumurtası* (testicles). Street stalls often sell *kokoreç*, an offal sausage.

Below: *Turks like their meat, so delicious sizzling kebabs are never far away*

Fish

Fish is abundant in Istanbul, but that doesn't mean it's cheap. *Barbunya* (red mullet), *sardalya* (sardines), *kefal* (grey mullet), fresh *palamut* (tuna), *kılıç* (swordfish), *sarıgöz* (bream), *lüfer* (blue fish), *Kalkan* (turbot), *hamsi* (anchovies), *levrek* (bass) and *karides* (prawns) are the most common fish and they are most often served grilled.

Wines and Drinks

Many Turks drink *ayran* (salted yoghurt drink) with their meal, and the choice of fresh fruit juices is abundant. Avoid tap water at all times; mineral water is widely available, either still or fizzy. Turkey produces some good red wines, including Yakut, Doluca and Dikmen, as well as white wines such as Çankaya and Kavak. Better and cheaper than the wine, however, is beer, especially Efes. Known as 'Lion's Milk', *rakı*, a grape spirit flavoured with aniseed, is one of the most popular drinks. It is similar to Greek *ouzo* but, unlike the Greeks, the Turks drink *rakı* with the meal, not as an aperitif.

Right: *strong, dark Turkish-style tea and coffee*

Coffee and Tea

The national drink is tea, grown along the Black Sea and served in small glasses any time of the day. Sugar comes on the side. Milk is never added. Although it was the Ottomans who introduced coffee into Europe, it is not widely drunk in Turkey. Turkish coffee, finely ground and brewed with sugar, is delicious, but Nescafé and Italian espresso are becoming increasingly common. Herbal teas such as *adaçay* (sage tea) and *ıhlamur* (linden flower) are not as popular as *elma çay* (apple tea).

Ortaköy Square, in the shadow of mosque and imposing bridge, makes for a pleasant excursion

+ 28B2
✉ Between Millet and Adnan Menderes (Vatan) Caddesi
🕐 Prayer hours
🚃 Tram from Sirkeci or Sultanahmet
♿ None
💷 Free
↔ Fenari İsa Camii (➤ 49)

MURAT PAŞA CAMİİ   ✪

This sombre mosque, now caught between heavy traffic, was built in 1470, shortly after the Ottoman conquest. Murat Paşa was born into the imperial Byzantine family but converted to Islam and became one of Sultan Mehmet's favourite generals. His mosque is interesting for the way it employs the Byzantine technique of alternating layers of brick and stone, while at the same time observing the Ottoman preoccupation with geometric forms.

+ 28B3
✉ Nişanca Caddesi, Fatih
🕐 Prayer hours
♿ None
💷 Free
↔ Fatih Camii (➤ 48)

NİŞANCI MEHMET PAŞA CAMİİ   ✪✪

The mosque of Mehmet Paşa, Keeper of the Seal (Nişancı) to Sultan Murat III, is approached through a lovely garden courtyard with an attractive central ablution fountain. It is a particularly beautiful building, of elegant proportions, completed in 1589. Inside, a grand central dome spans the prayer hall, resting on eight apses. Columns, capitals and cornice are all finely carved.

+ 38C3
✉ Nuruosmaniye Caddesi
🕐 Morning–evening
🚃 Tram stop Çemberlitaş
♿ None
💷 Free
↔ Kapalıçarşı (➤ 20), Atık Ali Paşa Camii (➤ 33), Çemberlitaş (➤ 43), Divan Yolu Caddesi (➤ 44), Mahmut Paşa Camii (➤ 57)

NURUOSMANİYE CAMİİ   ✪

The first baroque mosque in Istanbul, the Mosque of the Sacred Light of Osman set a pattern with the style and shape of its high central dome perched above the square prayer hall. The massive wheel-shaped arches that support this dome dominate the façade. Inside, above the gallery, runs a frieze carved with Koranic verses in a fine calligraphy. The complex, which includes a *medrese* (Islamic school), library, mausoleums and a *sebil* (fountain), was begun in 1748 by Sultan Mahmut I, but bears the name of his brother and successor, Osman III, who completed it in 1755. The courtyard is a delight.

ORTAKÖY ⊕⊕

The Ortaköy waterfront, in the shadow of the Bosphorus Bridge, is lined with bars and restaurants that in the evenings and during the Sunday market are packed with Istanbulis. The young so-called *entel*, or 'intellectuals', wander its narrow alleys looking for second-hand books, moderately priced antiques and crafts, or checking out the area's many trendy bars and restaurants. Dominating the seafront is the beautiful Ortaköy Camii, built for Sultan Abdülmecid I in 1854 by his favourite architect, Nikoğos Balyan, who also designed the Dolmabahçe Sarayı (► 45). Since 1973, the mosque has been dwarfed by the bridge; nevertheless, seen from the waterfront it provides an entrancing spectacle, its two fine minarets rising elegantly above the high dome over the prayer hall. The small Sinan Hamam, a good and cheaper alternative to the more famous *hamamı* (► 43) in Sultanahmet, is unfortunately closed at the time of writing.

PERA PALAS OTELİ ⊕⊕

Some major roads now surround the Pera Palace Hotel (it is just off İstiklâl Caddesi), but it is the splendour of the grand era of railway travel that the hotel's interior recalls. The Pera Palas was opened in 1892 by the Compagnie des Wagon-Lits to accommodate passengers travelling on the 'Orient Express' from Paris. As a hotel, it is now rather noisy and the service can be slow, but its appeal rests on nostalgia, not amenities. Atatürk's room (no. 101) has been turned into a permanent museum, but rooms in which other personalities and international stars stayed are available for rent: Greta Garbo slept in room 103, Ernest Hemingway preferred no. 218, Agatha Christie wrote part of *Murder on the Orient Express* in 401, 104 was Mata Hari's room and 304 was taken by Sarah Bernhardt. If you're not staying, at least have a drink (a Pera Palas cocktail, perhaps) or tea in the grand Orient Bar and sit admiring the pharaonic salons.

+ 82B2
⊠ European shore of the lower Bosphorus
🕐 Mosque prayer hours
🍴 Many bars and restaurants (mostly ££)
🚌 Bus 23b, 40 or 40b from Taksim, 25 or 22 from Eminönü
⛴ Ferry to Beşiktaş, and 15 minutes' walk
♿ Few
💲 Free
↔ Yıldız Parkı (► 78), Çırağan Palace Kempinski (► 102)
❓ Sunday junk and second-hand books market

Below: *be Hemingway for the afternoon and relax at the splendid bar of the Pera Palas Hotel*

+ 29D4
⊠ Meşrutiyet Caddesi 98
☎ 251 45 60; fax 251 40 89
🕐 Daily
🚇 Tünel
♿ Few
↔ Mevlevi Tekke (► 58)

Impressive Rumeli Hisarı is now a museum where theatrical performances are held in the summer

RAMAZAN EFENDİ CAMİİ ✪

Despite its elegant minaret, Ramazan Efendi's mosque has an uninviting exterior. Inside, it's another story: the prayer hall is completely covered in the finest İznik tiles. The bright red border tiles around the windows are particularly famous. The mosque is dubiously attributed to Mimar Sinan and was finished in 1586.

ROXELANA HAMAMI (HASEKİ HAMAMI) ✪✪

Built by Mimar Sinan in 1556 to replace the Byzantine baths of Zeuxippus, this is the second largest *hamam* in Turkey. Named after Süleyman's powerful wife Roxelana, it served as a *hamam* for worshippers at the nearby Aya Sofya (➤ 18). The 1980 restoration revealed plumbing problems that meant that it could no longer be used as a public bath. Since then, the Ministry of Culture has converted it into an exhibition space for hand-woven carpets, creating an easy way to see the interior of a bath without sweating. At the time of its construction the plan of the *hamam* was unusual for its symmetrical quarters for men and women, separated by a thick wall (which has since disappeared). After the bath visitors used to drink coffee and chat around the central fountain and beneath the magnificent dome of the *camekan* (reception and dressing hall). The second room was the tepid room (*soğukluk*) followed by the hot room (*hararet*) with its central massage platform; this one was heated. Washing was done near the basins by throwing buckets of water over the body.

> ## Did you know ?
>
> *Born in 1489 to a Christian family, Mimar Sinan entered the court of Selim I as a Janissary. At the age of 48 he was appointed imperial architect and it is believed that he designed 321 buildings, including 42 of Istanbul's mosques. Inspired and obsessed by the Byzantine Aya Sofya (➤ 18), he considered the Selimiye Mosque in Edirne (➤ 88) his masterpiece because the dome was larger than that of Justinian's great church. He died in 1588.*

RUMELİ HİSARI ✪✪

Magnificent Rumeli Castle commands the narrowest point of the Bosphorus. Mehmet the Conqueror had it built in just four months in 1452, facing the existing castle of Anadolu Hisarı (➤ 32). From here he was able to cut off Constantinople's supply of food from the Black Sea, a decisive factor in the Ottoman conquest of the city a year later. Restored in 1953, Rumeli, with its turrets and towers and thick, crenellated curtain walls, is an eloquent testimony to Ottoman military architecture.

✚ 82B3
✉ European shore of the Bosphorus
☎ 263 53 05
🕐 Tue–Sun 9:30–5
🍴 Ferry from Eminönü to Bebek, then bus
♿ None
💲 Moderate
↔ Anadolu Hisarı (➤ 32)

RÜSTEM PAŞA CAMİİ ✪✪✪

A small doorway from a busy street leads on to a dark stairway. There is little to prepare the visitor for the calm and splendour that lies beyond. This is another masterpiece designed by Sinan, in 1561, this time for Süleyman the Magnificent's Grand Vizier Rüstem Paşa. Called the Louse of Fortune, Rüstem Paşa was married to Süleyman's beloved daughter Mihrimah. The mosque is built on an awkward angle over several rows of shops, so from the benches on the terrace you can quietly watch the world go by, while the smells from the nearby Spice Bazaar (➤ 59) whet your appetite. Under the unusual double porch note the amazing blue and tomato-red İznik tiles on the walls, which date from the best period of İznik production (1550–1620). The prayer hall's bright and perfectly proportioned interior is decorated with more of these exquisite tiles from the kilns of master potters. Their geometric and floral patterns include carnations and red tulips on green leafed stems. Most of them were bought from İznik by Rüstem Paşa himself, although the tiling around the *mihrab* (prayer niche) appears to have been Sinan's choice.

✚ 38C4
✉ Hasırcılar Caddesi, Eminönü
🕐 Dawn–dusk
🚌 Buses to Galata Bridge, Eminönü
♿ None
↔ Süleymaniye Camii (➤ 22), Mısır Çarşısı (➤ 59)

Vivid colours of Rüstem Paşa Camii's interior

🕀 82B5
✉ Piyasa Caddesi 25–9, Büyükdere, European shore of the Bosphorus
☎ 242 38 13
🕐 Oct–Mar 10–5; Apr–Sep 10:30–6. Closed Wed
🍴 Cafeteria (£)
🚢 Ferry to Sarıyer and 10 minutes' walk
♿ None
💷 Moderate
🔁 Bosphorus (➤ 19 and 83)
❓ Museum shop sells excellent ceramics and books on Ottoman culture

SADBERK HANIM MÜZESİ ✪✪✪

The stunning collection of archaeological finds and Ottoman art is housed in a splendidly restored 19th-century wooden yalı (mansion). The white-painted, waterfront house is divided into two. The left wing is an archaeological museum, with objects arranged chronologically and attractively displayed against black marble. The artefacts bring to life Anatolian civilisation from the neolithic period to the Byzantine era. The first floor is devoted to Anatolian prehistory and includes amongst the exhibits a 7,500-year-old terracotta mother goddess curvaceous enough to catch the eye. The pottery jars burnished to look like metal are equally remarkable. Anatolia's entry into written history starts with clay tablets marked with cuneiform writing. On the half-landing there is a small display of hanging oil lamps and fine jewellery, including gold diadems crafted with olive leaves and flowers, while the second floor houses artefacts from the Mycenaean period to the early Byzantine. Some pottery shows an interesting fusion of Greek and local traditions, with classical vessels decorated with wild goat and plant motifs and marbling.

In the right wing the rooms of the yalı are restored to their former glory. The first floor houses one of the best collections of rare İznik tiles and Kütahya ceramics in İstanbul. The top floor illustrates life in the yalı and sheds some light on the customs of wealthy Ottomans with exhibits such as Rahmi Koç's bed where he rested after circumcision, a childbirth room and a collection of richly embroidered costumes.

🕀 38A3
✉ Şeyzadebaşi Caddesi, Saraçhane
🕐 Prayer hours
💷 Free
🔁 Bozdoğan Kemeri (➤ 40), Karikatür Müzesi (➤ 54)

ŞEHZADE CAMİİ ✪✪✪
(MOSQUE OF THE PRINCE)

Süleyman the Magnificent commissioned Sinan to build this grand complex in 1548 in memory of his eldest son Mehmet, who died of smallpox in 1543. This was Sinan's first imperial commission and it already shows the marks of his genius. One innovation was to conceal the buttresses behind colonnaded galleries on the north and

Left: *Mimar Sinan's grand Şehzade Camii*

south façade. The two minarets are finely decorated with bas-reliefs of geometric motifs, their balconies inlaid with terracotta. Inside, the mosque is unusually without columns, imposing rather than inspiring, though beautifully decorated with white calligraphy on a blue background. Prince Mehmet's garden tomb, also designed by Sinan, is exceptionally beautiful, as are the tombs of Rüstem Paşa and İbrahim Paşa. Across the garden is the elegant 18th-century *medrese* (Islamic school) of Damat İbrahim Paşa.

Far left: *a decorative late 16th-century tankard from the Sadberk Hanım Müzesi*

SELİMİYE KIŞLASI (SELIMIYE BARRACKS)   ✪

The massive building of the Selimiye Barracks is a distinctive feature on the Asian shore. The barracks were originally built by Selim III in 1800 for his Nizam-ı Cedid, or New Order, intended to undermine the power of the mutinous Janissary corps. The plan didn't work: the Janissaries smelt trouble, burned the building in 1808 and killed the sultan. The barracks were rebuilt in 1828, after Sultan Mahmud II's massacre of Janissaries, and were added to later by Sultan Abdülmecid. Today the building has more than 1,100 windows. During the Crimean War (1854–6) the barracks took their place in the history books when one wing was used as a hospital in which Florence Nightingale worked. Her rooms have been converted into a Florence Nightingale Museum displaying, amongst the original furnishings, some of her personal belongings and some pamphlets she wrote on nursing.

🚩 28B3
✉ Harem Feribot İskele
☎ 216-343 73 10
🕐 Closed for restoration at the time of writing.
🚢 Ferry from Sirkeci to Harem İskelesi
♿ None
💷 Free
🔁 Üsküdar (► 74–5)
❓ This is a military zone, so take your passport

The mosque's mushroom-like ablution fountain

29F2

Şehit Mehmet Paşa Yokuşu, Sultanahmet

Hours of prayer only; otherwise look for the *imam*, who has a key

None   Free

At Meydanı (► 17), Sultanahmet Camii (► 23), Küçük Ayasofya Camii (► 56), Mozaik Müzesi (► 59), Türk ve İslam Eserleri Müzesi (► 74)

SOKULLU MEHMET PAŞA CAMİİ

This is one of Istanbul's most beautiful small mosques, built for Sokullu Mehmet Paşa by Sinan in 1571. Sokullu Mehmet Paşa rose from a Janissary, through the ranks of the Ottoman court, to become the last Grand Vizier under Süleyman the Magnificent. He then married Esma, the daughter of Süleyman's successor, Selim II, and dedicated this jewel of a mosque to her. The approach is up a flight of stairs, under an impressive gateway, to a large courtyard surrounded by the rooms of a *medrese* (Islamic school), where you can still hear the murmur of boys studying the Koran.

Inside, beneath a high, elegant dome, there are some wonderful panels of beautiful İznik tiles on the east wall. White Koranic inscriptions on a blue background are boldly set in the middle of carnations and tulips depicted in vibrant red, green and blue. Uniquely, the designs and colours are repeated on the conical cap of the *mimbar* and elsewhere in the mosque, but otherwise the walls are left in simply carved white stone, which perfectly sets off the colours of the tiles. From the gallery, supported by arches resting on elegant marble columns, there are good views of the glorious tiles. Dark green pieces of stone, which are said to be from the Kaaba in Mecca, are inlaid above the entrance and in the *mimbar*, adding to the sanctity of the place.'

SPICE BAZAAR (MISIR ÇARŞISI) (► 59)

SÜLEYMANİYE CAMİİ (► 22, TOP TEN)

SULTANAHMET CAMİİ (► 23, TOP TEN)

39D1

At Meydanı, near the Sultanahmet Camii

Wed–Sun 9:30–4:30. Closed Mon, Tue

Tram stop Sultanahmet

Few

Donation welcome

At Meydanı (► 17), Sultanahmet Camii (► 23)

SULTANAHMET TÜRBESİ

Sultan Ahmet I died aged only 28, just a year after supervising the construction of the Blue Mosque (► 23). His *türbe*, which forms part of the mosque complex, was completed by his son, Sultan Osman II. Osman was overthrown by Janissaries just five years after Ahmet's death and was put to death by having his testicles crushed. His brother Murat IV is also buried here. The recently restored tomb consists of a square chamber decorated with late İznik tiles, not of the same quality as in the mosque; eight hanging arches support a fine dome.

SULTAN MAHMUT II TÜRBESİ ✪

Appropriately for a sultan who helped Westernise the Empire, Sultan Mahmut II's mausoleum, dating from 1838, was built in French Empire style. A grand chandelier hangs from the marble dome. The tombs, belonging to the sultan and his family, including sultans Abdul Aziz and Abdul Hamit II, are wrapped in rich velvet.

➕ 39E2
✉ Divan Yolu Caddesi
🕐 Tue–Sun 9:30–4:30. Closed Mon
🚋 Tram stop Çemberlitaş
💵 Free
↔ Divan Yolu (➤ 44)

SULTAN SELİM CAMİİ ✪✪

The mosque of Selim I, 'the Grim', crowns Istanbul's Fifth Hill, towering over the Haliç (Golden Horn). Built by Süleyman the Magnificent in 1522 in memory of his father, it is still one of the city's finest buildings. The courtyard is a delight, ringed by 18 polychrome arches supported by antique marble and granite columns. The domed ablution fountain stands amongst cypress trees. Lunettes above the windows are decorated with superb early İznik tiles. The interior was kept simple, perhaps in tune with the sultan's character, and the decoration of the *mihrab* (prayer niche), *mimbar* (pulpit) and sultan's *loge* is restrained. In the enclosed garden are the tombs of Selim I and some of his grandchildren, as well as that of the 19th-century sultan Abdülmecid I.

➕ 39D2
✉ Yavuz Selim Caddesi, Fatih
🕐 Mosque: prayer hours. Tomb: Wed–Sun 9:30–4:30
⛴ Ferry from Eminönü to Aykapı İskelesi, 15 minutes' walk
♿ None
💵 Free
↔ Bulgar Kilise (➤ 41), Fethiye Camii (➤ 49)

The grand and spacious mosque of Sultan Selim I

TAKSİM MEYDANI (TAKSİM SQUARE) ✪✪✪

A vast beating, blaring square lined with ugly concrete high-rise blocks and dominated by a bus station and fast-food restaurants, Taksim Meydanı may have lost its soul, but it remains the heart of modern Istanbul. The square takes its name from an 18th-century octagonal reservoir (*taksim*), near the French Consulate on İstiklâl Caddesi (► 53), which provided water for the city's modern quarters. The square's central Monument to the War of Independence was designed by an Italian sculptor in 1928 to celebrate the heroes who created modern Turkey, Atatürk amongst them. On the east side of the square is the glass-fronted Atatürk Cultural Centre, home to the Istanbul Opera. North of the square, along Cumhuriyet Caddesi, the Municipal Art Gallery houses a collection of paintings of Istanbul by Turkey's best artists. Cumhuriyet Caddesi leads further north into more attractive and affluent shopping and residential areas: Harbiye, Maçka, Şişli and Nişantaşı.

🕂 29D4
✉ Taksim Meydanı
🍽 Many fast-food restaurants (£)
🚋 Tramway from Tünel
♿ Good
🎫 Free
↔ İstiklâl Caddesi (► 53)

Elaborate geometrical patterns in the brickwork of the now ruined Tekfur Sarayı

🕂 28B4
✉ Hoca Çakır Caddesi, Edirnekapı, Fatih
🕐 All day
🚌 Bus 86 from Eminönü
♿ Few; none on walls
🎫 Free; small tip for guardian
↔ Kariye Camii (► 21), Mihrimah Camii (► 58), Theodosian Walls (► 71)

TEKFUR SARAYI (PALACE OF THE SOVEREIGN) ✪✪

The late 13th-century Byzantine Tekfur Sarayı, the Palace of the Porphyrogenitus, is a ruin, but the surviving walls suggest it was once an impressive three-storey building. Polychrome arches decorate the windows, while the façade is striped with geometrical patterns in white marble and red brick. Only the third floor appeared above the Theodosian land walls (► 71). From the top of the walls you get a good idea of the spectacular views that would have been enjoyed from its windows. The palace appears to have been an annexe of nearby Blachernae Palace, the main Byzantine imperial palace. After the Ottoman conquest it housed the Sultan's menagerie of elephants and giraffes and subsequently was used for workshops before it fell into ruin.

THEODOSIAN WALLS (TEODOS II SURU) ✪✪✪

The 6.5km-long walls that defended Istanbul on its land side, stretching from the Sea of Marmara to the Golden Horn, were named after Theodosius II, though he was only a teenager when construction started in AD 413. The first part of the new wall, built to accommodate the growing city of Constantinople, was almost completely destroyed by an earthquake, leaving the city defenceless against the advancing armies of Attila the Hun. As reconstruction had to happen in a hurry, every citizen, regardless of status, was forced to help. An inscription at the restored Mevlana Kapı (gate) reads: 'By the command of the Emperor Theodosius II, the prefect Constantine erected these strong walls in less than two months'. The original walls were 5m thick and 12m high, flanked by an outer wall 2m thick and 8.5m high, a 20m-wide moat and 96 towers. For 1,000 years these walls protected the city. They were finally breached on 29 May 1453 by Mehmet II; many historians cite this date as the end of the Middle Ages. The Theodosian Walls are now a UNESCO World Heritage Site and sections are being thoroughly restored.

Walking the full length of the walls is only for the energetic and will take most of a day. Start at Yedikule (➤ 76) and walk along the walls to Yedikule Kapı. A path along the top of the inner wall leads to the Belgrade Kapı, where a cannon ball remains stuck in the wall from the time of Mehmet II. From here, walk through the grave-yards east of the walls to Silivri Kapı and continue through the back streets, following the wall to Mevlana Kapı. The next stretch of walls has been taken over by gypsy camps, so continue along the streets to Topkapı (more cannon balls). Adnan Menderes (Vatan) Caddesi runs further on towards the Edirnekapı where the walls end, past Tekfur Sarayı (➤ 70) at newly laid-out gardens near the Golden Horn. The areas around the walls are not the most salubrious: dress modestly and avoid wearing jewellery.

➕ 39F3
✉ Yedikule, Topkapı, Edirnekapı
🕐 All day
🚌 Buses from Eminönü no. 80 to Yedikule, 86 to Edirnekapi and 84 to Topkapi
♿ None
👆 Free
↔ Tekfur Sarayı (➤ 70), Kariye Camii (➤ 21), Koca Mustafa Paşa Camii (➤ 55), Mihrimah Camii (➤ 58), Yedikule (➤ 76)

The well-preserved Gate of Christ, set in the Theodosian Walls

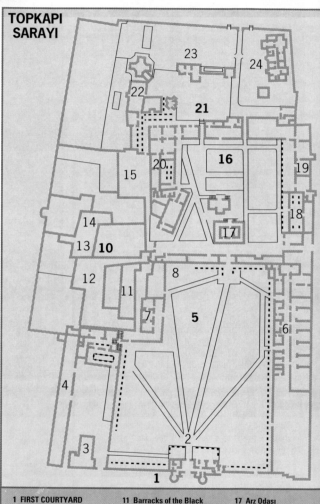

TOPKAPI SARAYI

1 **FIRST COURTYARD**
2 Orta Kapı
3 Beşir Ağa Camii
4 Stables
5 **SECOUND COURTYARD**
6 Palace Kitchens
7 Divan
8 Inner Treasury
9 Babüssade
10 **HAREM**

11 Barracks of the Black Eunuchs
12 Apartments of Principal Wives
13 Apartments of Valide Sultan
14 Hünkar Sofası
15 Apartments of Favourite Wives
16 **THIRD COURTYARD**

17 Arz Odası
18 Seferi Koğuşu
19 Pavilion of the Conqueror
20 Pavilion of the Holy Mantle
21 **FOURTH COURTYARD**
22 Marble Terrace
23 Sofa Köşkü
24 Mecidiye Köşkü

Through the Topkapı Palace Grounds

From the Bab-ı Hümayun (also ➤ 24–5), walk through the First Courtyard and buy a ticket (on your right).

Walk through the Orta Kapı, and follow the path left across the Second Courtyard.

Buy another ticket for a guided tour of the Harem immediately, as tickets are limited. The Divan is where the council met. The sultan used to overhear their deliberations through a window grille known as the 'Eye of the Sultan'. The Treasury houses the Arms and Armour Collection.

Proceed through the Babüssaade or the Gate of Felicity to the Third Courtyard.

Straight ahead is the Throne Room where the sultan listened to the outcome of the Divan meetings.

Walk towards the right.

The Pavilion of the Conqueror houses the spectacular Topkapı Treasury.

Walk straight across the courtyard to the Pavilion of the Holy Mantle.

Here the most precious Muslim relics are stored. These include the Holy Mantle, the hair and sword of Prophet Muhammad and Moses' stick. Next door is the Topkapı's Collection of Paintings and Miniatures.

Walk through the passageway to the Fourth Courtyard and turn left.

The Marble Terrace offers magnificent views over Istanbul. Its 17th-century Bağdat Köşkü has an amazing tiled interior. Across the courtyard is the Mecidiye Köşkü with the excellent Konyalı restaurant (➤ 93) and a cafeteria, both overlooking the Bosphorus and Galata. On the way back, look to the left of the Second Courtyard into the vast Palace Kitchens.

Distance
1km

Time
Easily half a day

Start/end point
✚ 39E2
🚊 Tram stop Sultanahmet

Lunch
Cafeteria (£–££) or Konyalı Restaurant (£££) in the Fourth Courtyard (➤ 93).

Great views over Istanbul from the Marble Terrace near Bağdat Köşkü in the Fourth Courtyard

TOPKAPI SRARYI (► 24–5, TOP TEN)

TÜRK VE İSLAM ESERLERİ MÜZESİ ✪✪✪

In 1523, when İbrahim Paşa, Grand Vizier and lifelong friend of Süleyman, completed his palace, it was the largest house in the Ottoman Empire, grander even than Topkapı (► 24–5) – which perhaps accounts for the campaign that Roxelana, Süleyman's wife, waged against him. İbrahim Paşa was eventually killed on the sultan's orders. The remains of the house were restored in the 1960s as a Museum of Turkish and Islamic Art (7th–19th centuries). Manuscripts, pottery, calligraphy, carved wood, metalwork and stained glass are arranged chronologically, which helps you understand the shift from Ummayad, through Abbasid, Mameluk, Selçuk and Beylik to Ottoman style. The highlights include Selçuk tiles with floral patterns – made in Konya but obviously the precedent for İznik ware – and exquisite 16th-century miniatures. More memorable are the Turkish carpets, one of the world's finest collections, including some named after European painters, who used them in paintings, and also a carpet decorated with a double tiger stripe.

On the courtyard level there is an equally well-displayed ethnographic collection from nomadic Yoruks from Anatolia, including clothing and lamb-skin tents. There are great views over Sultanahmet Camii (► 23) from the lovely courtyard café.

➕ 39D2
✉ At Meydanı 46, Sultanahmet
☎ 518 19 06
🕐 Tue–Sun 9–4:30
🍴 Cafeteria (£) in courtyard
♿ None
▦ Moderate
⟷ At Meydanı (► 17), Sultanahmet Camii (► 23), Binbirdirek Sarnıç (► 36)

Turkish rugs like these have inspired artists such as Van Eyck and Bellini

ÜSKÜDAR ✪✪

Üsküdar is the Asian face of Istanbul, but as it is only a 15-minute ferry ride from Eminönü, you shouldn't expect a world of difference. Although now an important district of Istanbul, during the Ottoman period it was outside the city walls. At that time it was considered a good thing for Constantinople's rich and famous to build mosques and religious foundations on the Asian shore, and there is, as a result, a concentration of mosques, starting right by the ferry landing. From the square-shaped Hakimiyet-i Milliye Meydanı, the 'Sacred Caravan' set off for Mecca – white camels loaded with gifts from the sultan and a long line of pilgrims. The square – and the baroque fountain in the middle – is dominated by the Mihrimah Sultan Camii

➕ 82B1
✉ Asian shore of the lower Bosphorus
🕐 Mosques open during prayer hours
🍴 Several restaurants and cafés near the pier (£)
🚢 Boats from Eminönü pier no.1 to Üsküdar
♿ None
▦ Free
⟷ Selimiye Kışlası (► 67)

(1548), also known as the Iskele Camii (Mosque of the Landing), the first of two mosques Sinan built for the daughter of Süleyman the Magnificent. Across the square is the Yeni Valide Camii, built in 1710 by Ahmet III for his mother, with a lovely tree-shaded courtyard. The valide sultan's tomb is covered with roses. The pretty limestone mosque on the

> ### *Did you know ?*
>
> *The Karaca Ahmet Mezarlığı, on the road from Üsküdar to Kadıköy, is one of the largest cemeteries in the Orient, a vast and peaceful forest of tombs. Istanbulis come to the city's cemeteries for a stroll or a picnic, and to offer perfume, milk or flowers to the deceased. Find other cemeteries outside the land walls, at Eyüp and around the mosques.*

waterfront is Şemsi Paşa Camii, built by Sinan for a vizier of Süleyman the Magnificent. Just behind it stands a 15th-century mosque built like a Byzantine church: the Rum Mehmet Paşa Camii was built by a Greek, Mehmet Paşa, who converted to Islam. Further along the waterfront towards Kadıköy is the 18th-century Ayazma Camii, a lovely baroque mosque built near a sacred spring by Mustafa III for his mother. About 200m offshore is one of the landmarks that has come to symbolise the Bosphorus, the Kız Kulesi (Maiden's Tower), a white tower set on a tiny island. The island has served as fortification, quarantine and customs post, but is named after the legend of a sultan's daughter who was locked in the tower after a prediction that she would die from a snake bite. When she was offered a basket of fruit containing a snake, the prophecy came true.

Ferries plying the route between Eminönü and Üsküdar pass close to the Maiden's Tower

75

Yedikule, scene of the murder of Osman II

YEDİKULE (CASTLE OF THE SEVEN TOWERS) ✪✪✪

The Byzantine gateway of Yedikule Kapı, once the most important of the 18 city gates, leads to Yedikule, the Castle of the Seven Towers. A curious building, incorporating Byzantine and Ottoman elements – an indicator of its 1,600 year-long history – it has now been turned into a museum. The Golden Gate (Altın Kapı), a huge triumphal arch flanked by two marble towers set into the west wall, was built by Theodosius I in 390 and originally stood alone on a hill. The gate took its name from its gold-plated doors and gilded statues; only emperors and visiting foreign rulers were allowed to ride through it. Yediküle's other five towers were added by Mehmet the Conqueror when he turned it into a fortress. Despite appearances, it was never used as a castle, but served as a state prison and treasury. The cells of the Golden Gate were the scene of some bloody executions, including that of the 18-year-old Sultan Osman II, who was tortured and hanged here.

YENİ CAMİ (NEW MOSQUE) ✪

Officially known as the Yeni Valide Sultan Camii, the New Mosque is so called because it is 'only' 400 years old. Because of its proximity to the bazaars, bus station and ferry landings, this grand mosque, which dominates your view as you approach from the Galata Bridge, seems more approachable than some. A broad flight of steps, often colonised by pigeons, leads to a monumental gateway. The porticoed courtyard contains antique columns and a pretty, hexagonal ablution fountain. The prayer hall is a perfect square, with sections of the walls decorated in what are, for Istanbul, dull İznik tiles.

YEREBATAN SARAYI (➤ 26, TOP TEN)

From Eminönü to Taksim Meydanı

Start at Yeni Cami (▶ 76) and cross to the left side of the Galata (Karaköy) Bridge.

From the bridge walk straight ahead along the steep pavement, and at Voyvoda Caddesi with its grand façades, turn left. Take Yüksek Kaldırım Caddesi or the first alley to the right and climb the monumental stairway that leads to the Galata Tower (▶ 50).

The second alley to the right off Voyvoda Caddesi leads into the brothel area, so don't miss that first turning!

After the visit turn right and walk across the square. Then turn left and left again on Galip Dede Caddesi.

After 200m, the Mevlevi Tekke is on the right (▶ 58). Continue along this street, many of whose shops sell musical instruments, until the end. Turn right on İstiklâl Caddesi (▶ 53). The second street to the left, Asmalı Mescit Sokak leads to the famous Pera Palas Oteli (Pera Palace Hotel) (▶ 63).

Return to the main street.

No. 429 is the Church of St Maria Draperis, no. 327 the Basilica of St Anthony, while further along on the small square is the Imperial Lyceum of Galatasaray, where for years the élite of Turkish society were educated. Past the square is the famous Çiçek Pasajı, with its sign, 'Cité de Pera'.

Walk through and bear left. Cross the Fish Market (Balık Pazarı) into the beautifully restored Avrupa Pasajı. At the end turn right and immediately take the Aslıhane Pasajı, lined with bookstores.

Stroll around in the market and return to the main street to reach Taksim Meydanı.

Distance
2.5km

Time
3–4 hours

Start point
✚ 39D4
🚌 All buses to Eminönü

End point
✚ 29D4
🚌 Tünel tramway

Refreshment
Tea at the Pera Palas Oteli (▶ 63), profiteroles at İnci (▶ 97), tea and Turkish delights at Hacı Bekir (▶ 97) or lunch at Hacı Abdullah (▶ 92–3).

Everything is on the move in the busy area of İstiklâl Caddesi

🔲 29F5

✉️ Çırağan Caddesi,
European shore of lower
Bosphorus, between
Beşiktaş and Ortaköy

☎️ 260 80 60

🕐 Daily 8:30–5:30 (Şale
Köşkü: Wed–Sun 9:30–4.
Closed Mon, Tue. Guided
tours only)

🍴 Cafeterias (£)

🚢 Beşiktaş Vapur İskelesi
(ferry landing)

♿ None

🎫 Park: free. Şale
Köşkü: moderate

🔁 Çırağan Palace Kempinski
(➤ 102), Ortaköy (➤ 63)

YILDIZ PARKI (YILDIZ PARK) ✪✪✪

This popular public park, a vast area of enclosed woodland dotted with pavilions, statues, gardens and lakes, once formed the imperial Yıldız Palace gardens. The palace and park were built by Sultan Abdühamid II, who reigned from here over the crumbling empire between 1876 and 1909. Being paranoid, he had many tunnels and cellars dug underground – now covered by the park. Both the park and the *köşks* (pavilions) were restored by the Turkish Touring Club in 1979.

Şale Köşkü, a copy of a Swiss Chalet, is the most impressive building to have survived. It was built to entertain the visiting Kaiser Wilhelm II in 1889. Guided tours reveal an ornate 19th-century interior with lovely painted wood panelling, a mother-of-pearl inlaid drawing room, chairs made by the sultan himself and a 400sq m Hereke carpet in the celebration hall.

Right: *Ottoman-style fittings inside the Sale Köşkü*

Far right: *a wonderfully decorated vault in Kariye Camii*

🔲 38A5

✉️ İbadethane Sokaşı, off
Atatürk Bulvarı, Unkapanı

🕐 Prayer hours only, but the
imam will open the door
for a small tip

♿ None

🎫 Free

🔁 Bozdoğan Kemeri
(➤ 40), Karikatür Müzesi
(➤ 54), also Walk (➤ 42)

ZEYREK CAMİİ (CHURCH OF THE PANTOCRATOR) ✪

John II Comnenus and Empress Irene of Hungary built this 12th-century church, originally two churches connected by a chapel, as a family mausoleum. There is no trace of the nearby monastery, also founded by the saintly Empress Irene, which became one of the largest in the empire. For three centuries, emperors were buried here, but their tombs were removed soon after the Ottoman conquest, when it was converted into a mosque. Inside, there are some mosaics in the south aisle and a triple marble door, but otherwise little original decoration has survived. A marble medallion of Samson is covered with carpet, which the guardian, with a little persuasion, will lift.

Istanbul Excursions

Istanbul has much to offer, but not in the way of peace and quiet or fresh air. If that's what you're looking for, then you'll need to escape and the easiest way to do that is either to cruise on the Bosphorus or to walk in the Belgrade Forest. The nearby Princes' Islands are peaceful and there are some wonderful 19th-century *yalıs* for rent, but be aware that in summer thousands will be joining you in search of a cool breeze. The best beaches near Istanbul are Kilyos and Şile on the Black Sea. Istanbulis all seem to want to leave the city at the same moment, especially at the weekend, when traffic can be a nightmare. To escape the crowds, for rural scenery, forests, fresh mountain air and excellent hiking, head for the mountains, not far from Istanbul. In winter, skiing is only a long day trip away, at Uludağ, one of Turkey's premier ski resorts. And if you haven't had your fill of Ottoman architecture, look for some early examples in Edirne, Bursa or İznik.

' The pleasure of going in a barge to Chelsea is not comparable to that of rowing up on the Canal of the Sea here '

Lady Mary Wortley Montagu,
Letter to Lady Bristol,
10 April 1718

Belgrad Ormanı &
European Boğaziçi

Starting at Taksim, head north on the highway to Büyükdere.

Just past Büyükdere follow signposts left for Bahçeköy, on the eastern edge of the Belgrad Ormanı (Belgrade Forest) (► 84).

Along the main road find the ruined village of Belgrad and two of the most impressive aqueducts built by Sinan for Süleyman.

Follow the signs to Sarıyer (► 90), back on the Boğaziçi (Bosphorus).

Walk along the seafront, past well-preserved *yalıs*, and visit the wonderful Sadberk Hanım Müzesi (► 66).

Return to Istanbul, following the pretty coastal road, lined with good fish restaurants.

The next village after Sarıyer is Tarabya, where many foreign diplomats have their summer homes. There are more fish restaurants here, of which Deniz (► 98) is reputedly one of the best. After İstinye, Emirgan is famous for its Tulip Garden. (Tulips were first exported from Turkey to Holland in the 17th century.) In the middle of the park, which is best seen in spring, are three 19th-century kiosks, restored as excellent cafés, and a concert hall. Beyond the magnificent span of the Fatih Sultan Mehmet Köprüsü, built in 1988 and currently ranked as the world's third longest suspension bridge, is the majestic Rumeli Hisarı (► 65).

The road continues to the wealthy suburb of Bebek.

Splendid mansions line the waterfront. In the shadow of the next bridge lies the increasingly popular district of Ortaköy (► 63), from where the road leads back to Beşiktaş past Yıldız Parkı (► 78).

Distance
75km

Time
5–6 hours

Start point
✚ 29E4

End point
✚ 82B2

Refreshment
Have lunch at one of the fish restaurants along the way (► 98) and end with tea at one of the lovely kiosks or conservatories in Yıldız Parkı.

The Rumeli Hisarı commands stunning views of the Bosphorus and the Anadolu Hisarı

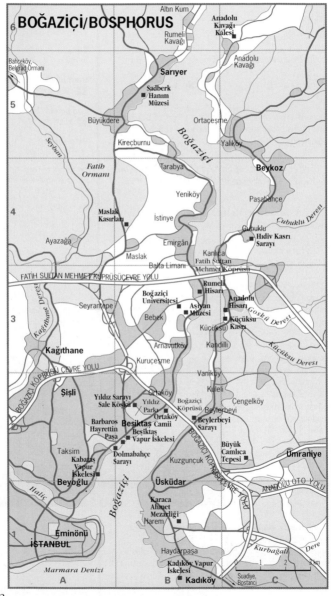

BOĞAZİÇİ/BOSPHORUS

Altın Kum

Rumeli
Kavağı

Anadolu
Kavağı Kalesi

Anadolu
Kavağı

Bahçeköy,
Belgrad Ormanı

Sarıyer

**Sadberk
Hanım
Müzesi**

Büyükdere

Ortaçeşme

Boğaziçi

Kireçburnu

Yalıköy

Seyhan

*Fatih
Ormanı*

Tarabya

Beykoz

Yeniköy

Paşabahçe

Çubuklu Deresi

**Maslak
Kasırları**

İstinye

Çubuklu

**Hıdiv Kasrı
Sarayı**

Ayazağa

Emirgân

Kanlıca

Maslak

Balta Limanı

Fatih Sultan
Mehmet Köprüsü

FATİH SULTAN MEHMET KÖPRÜSÜ ÇEVRE YOLU

**Rumeli
Hisarı**

**Boğaziçi
Üniversitesi**

**Anadolu
Hisarı**

Seyrantepe

**Aşiyan
Müzesi**

Göksu Deresi

Bebek

**Küçüksu
Kasrı**

Küçüksu

Kağıthane

Arnavutköy

Kandilli

Küçüksu Deresi

Kuruçeşme

Kağıthane Deresi

Vaniköy

Kuleli

Şişli

**Yıldız Sarayı
Şale Köşkü**

Ortaköy

**Yıldız
Parkı**

Boğaziçi
Köprüsü

Çengelköy

**Ortaköy
Camii**

Beylerbeyi

**Barbaros
Hayrettin
Paşa**

Beşiktaş

**Beşiktaş
Vapur İskelesi**

**Beylerbeyi
Sarayı**

BOĞAZİÇİ KÖPRÜSÜ ÇEVRE YOLU

Taksim

**Büyük
Çamlıca
Tepesi**

**Kabataş
Vapur
İskelesi**

**Dolmabahçe
Sarayı**

Kuzguncuk

Ümraniye

Beyoğlu

Boğaziçi

Üsküdar

ANADOLU OTO YOLU

Haliç

**Karaca
Ahmet
Mezarlığı**

Harem

Eminönü

İSTANBUL

Haydarpaşa

Kurbağalı

Dere

**Kadıköy Vapur
İskelesi**

Marmara Denizi

Suadiye,
Bostancı

1 2 3 km

A **B ■ Kadıköy** **C**

The Asian Side of the Boğaziçi

The easiest way to see the sights on the Asian shore is by taxi. Admire palaces and fortresses on the way and cruise back from the last ferry stop.

Leave from Beyoğlu over the old Boğaziçi (Bosphorus) suspension bridge.

Just beside the bridge is the 19th-century Beylerbeyi Sarayı (➤ 36). Continue along the coast road to Çengelköy, watching out for the well-preserved Kırmızı Yalı and the baroque fountain in the square. Past the village is Kuleli, a famous officers' training school and the smaller of two hospitals that Florence Nightingale ran during the Crimean War. Continue to the rococo Küçüksu Kasrı palace (➤ 56) and walk from there to the ruined castle of Anadolu Hisarı (➤ 32). Kanlıca, further north, is renowned for its yoghurt served with icing sugar.

Past the village, follow the signpost uphill for Çubuklu.

On top of the hill stands the palace of the former khedive of Egypt, Hıdiv Kasrı, transformed into a luxury hotel by the Turkish Touring Club (closed at the time of writing).

Return to the main road and continue north.

Pasabahçe has a large *rakı* distillery where you may sample the drink. Carry on to Beykoz and admire the splendid *yalı* of Mehmet Ali Paşa. Anadolu Kavağı is the last stop for cruise boats. Check the timetables on arrival, then decide if there is time for a fish lunch or the climb to the castle of Murat IV, which dominates the village. Cruise back to Istanbul.

Distance
70km

Time
5–6 hours depending on the frequency of ferries

Start point
➕ 82B2

End point
➕ 82A1

Lunch
Best at Çengelköy or at Anadolu Kavağı (both have many fish restaurants)

Cruising practicalities
Several ferries (*vapur*) leave daily from pier no. 3, indicated as Boğaz Hattı, at Eminönü. Timetables are available at the ticket office and tickets are cheap. It takes about 1hr 45mins to reach the last stop on the Bosphorus, at Anadolu Kavağı. Ferries stop at several piers on the way: Barbaros Hayrettin Paşa, Yeniköy, Sarıyer, Rumeli Kavağı on the European side, Kanlıca and Anadolu Kavağı in Asia. You can hop off and catch the next ferry, but check timetables first and remember that you will need a new ticket.

Cruising is a relaxing way to explore the villages, palaces and restaurants along the Bosphorus

86C2

About 20–30km from
Istanbul, in the Sea of
Marmara (Marmara
Denizi)

Kalpazankaya Gazinosu
on Burgazada ☎ 216 -
381 15 04
Kaptan Lokantası and
Yörük Ali Restaurant on
Büyükada (➤ 98)

Cheap regular ferries
from Sirkeci pier no. 5
marked Adalar (less than
2 hours to the furthest
island) or less regular but
faster sea bus (Deniz
Otobüsü) from Kabataş
pier

None

Above: *small boats line
the harbour of
Heybeliada, one of the
Princes' Islands*

86C2

20km from Istanbul on
European shore

Tea house at Neşet Suyu

Ferry from Eminönü to
Sarıyer or Büyükdere and
a dolmuş from Çayırbaşi
near Büyükdere to
Bahçeköy

Sadberk Hanım Müzesi
(➤ 66), Sarıyer (➤ 90)

ADALAR (PRINCES' ISLANDS) ✪✪✪

The Princes' Islands have become a favourite retreat from
Istanbul, and many families move here during the summer
months, commuting to the city. The islands are still a
pedestrian zone, except for the occasional horse-drawn
carriage. As ferry services increase, there is a growing risk
of over-development, which might spoil the islands' beauty
and quiet.

The islands were named back in the Byzantine era
when princes and empresses no longer welcome at court
took refuge in the many monasteries founded here. Until
the 19th century the islands remained a place of exile, and
even in 1961 the smaller Sivriada served as a prison for the
deposed prime minister Adnan Menderes, who was later
hanged there.

Büyükada, the largest island and the furthest away from
Istanbul, is also the most visited. Horse-drawn carriages by
the pier do a long or short tour (➤ 85) of the island,
passing some of the most magnificent wooden *konaks*, or
summer houses, and the sandy coves. The northern hill is
crowned by the empty Monastery of the Transfiguration,
while the large and beautiful Monastery of St George sits
on the other hill. Both Burgazada and Heybeliada have
good beaches for swimming.

BELGRAD ORMANI (BELGRADE FOREST) ✪✪

Istanbul's lungs, the Belgrade Forest, is the only woodland
near the city worth the name. A famous hunting ground in
Ottoman times and a playground for the city's foreign
community, the forest was named after workers brought
from Belgrade in 1521 by Süleyman the Magnificent to
oversee the elaborate water system. There is still plenty of
evidence of reservoirs and fragments of aqueducts all over
the place – worth exploring during your walk. The most
impressive is the Long Aqueduct (Uzun Kemer), built in
1563 by Sinan.

Fayton (Phaeton) Ride Around Büyükada

Leave Istanbul in the morning and take the ferry from Adalar İskelesi, opposite Sirkeci train station in Eminönü. Several ferries a day stop at all the large islands (1½–2 hours to Büyükada). The tour of the southern part of the island can be made on foot, but it is often more fun to cycle (hire bikes in the little square near the Princess Hotel). Otherwise take the *Büyük Tur*, or Big Tour, by horse-and-carriage (quite expensive).

With your back to the sea leave the square to the right on the steep road. At the end turn left into a street with several exceptional yalıs *and villas, and then right on Çankaya Caddesi, which has even grander constructions.*

Note, amongst many, the elegant Italian villa Baharı to the left, which is being turned into a hotel by the Turkish Touring Club.

Continue along Nizam Caddesi, which goes down to Dilburnu Ormanizi, a lovely pine forest and picnic area overlooking the sea. Keep on, following horse-and-carriages on the main road, and at the Luna Park follow the signpost right for Büyük Tur.

If the views of the clear sea and the perfumes of pine, fresh herbs and wild flowers make you feel like swimming, try the tiny footpaths along the way or ask a carriage driver. Further on, the road is lined with horse stables, as the smell indicates.

At the fork follow the coastal road to the left to another residential area with more fantastic wooden villas. Return through the main street to the ferry landing.

Distance
6km

Time
3 hours' walk, 1 hour by carriage and 2 hours by bike, not including time for a picnic

Start/end point
✚ 39D4
🚢 Ferry from Adalar İskelesi in Eminönü or the faster waterbus from the Kabataş landing.

Lunch
Buy food for a picnic in the market street to the left of the ferry landing and eat it in the picnic area.

Büyükada has stunning scenery and is perfumed by mastic and pine trees and fragrant herbs

85

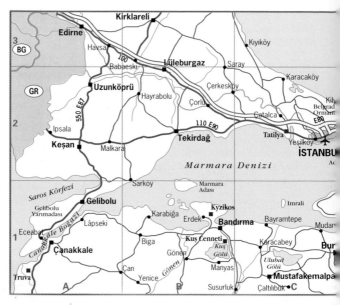

<table>
<tr><td>⊞</td><td>86C1</td></tr>
<tr><td>✉</td><td>243km from Istanbul</td></tr>
<tr><td>🕐</td><td>Muradiye: Tue–Sun
8:30–12, 1–5. Yeşil Türbe:
daily 8–12, 1–5.
Archaeological Museum:
Tue–Sun 8:30–12, 1–5:30</td></tr>
<tr><td>🍽</td><td>İskender (£), Cumurcul
(££) (➤ 99)</td></tr>
<tr><td>🚌</td><td>Bus from Istanbul
Topkapı Otogar (4 hours)</td></tr>
<tr><td>ℹ</td><td>Tourist Office, Ulu Camii
Parkı, Heykel ☎ 224-
220 18 48</td></tr>
<tr><td>♿</td><td>None</td></tr>
<tr><td>↔</td><td>Uludağ (➤ 90)</td></tr>
<tr><td>❓</td><td>Hamamı: ask directions
and timetables from the
tourist office. Late
Jun/Jul cocoon auction at
the Koza Han</td></tr>
</table>

Far right: *the interior of
Bursa's Green Mosque*

BURSA ●●●

'Green Bursa', set on the lower slopes of Uludağ, is a vibrant modern city that offers some of the finest early Ottoman monuments in Turkey. Bursa was the first capital of the Ottoman Empire and the first six sultans are buried at the Muradiye complex, built in 1424 by Murad II. Set in a well-kept garden, most of the tombs, including the splendid *türbe* of Murad II, are lavishly decorated with İznik tiles, as is the Muradiye Mosque. The nearby Kültür Parkı has a boating lake, cafés and restaurants. Here too is the local Archaeological Museum. At the heart of Bursa is the Koza Parkı, with fountains and cafés, and Beyazıt I's 14th-century Ulu Camii, notable for its limestone façade and exquisite walnut *mimbar* (pulpit). Near the early 14th-century Orhan Gazi Camii are the Koza Hanı, where farmers sell cocoons to make silk – a speciality of Bursa – and the Bedesten, the bazaar where the famous Bursa towels are for sale. Across the stream is the Yeşil Cami (Green Mosque), Bursa's most spectacular mosque, sumptuously decorated with green-turquoise tiles. Bursa has been renowned for thermal baths since Roman times. Check out the beautiful *hamamı*, particularly the Eski Kapilca, which dates to the time of Justinian.

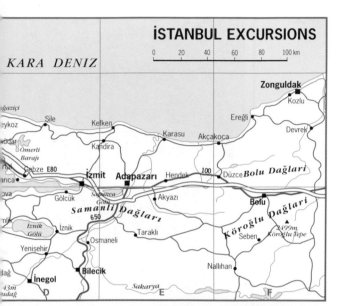

İSTANBUL EXCURSIONS

0   20   40   60   80   100 km

KARA DENIZ

Zonguldak
Kozlu
Ereğli
Devrek

Şile   Kefken   Karasu   Akçakoca
eykoz
dar   Kandira
Ömerli
Barajı
abze E80   İzmit   Adapazarı   Hendek   100   Düzce   Bolu Dağları
rica
ova
Gölcük   Sapanca   Akyazı   Bolu
Gölü
İznik   Samanlı Dağları   650   Köroğlu Dağları
Gölü   İznik   Taraklı   Seben   2499m
Yenişehir   Osmaneli   Köroğlu Tepe

dağ   İnegöl   Bilecik   Nallıhan
43m
udağ   D   Sakarya   E   F

The introduction of the large dome marked a turning point in Ottoman architecture

86A3

250km from Istanbul, on the border with Greece and Bulgaria

Selimiye Tue–Sun 9–12, 2–5 (2–7 in winter)

Aile Restaurant (£), near the post office, Saraçlar Caddesi. Closed Sun

Bus from Topkapı Otogar, Istanbul

Hürriyet Meydanı, Londra Asfaltı
☎ 284-225 15 18

None

Kirkpinar (oil-wrestling festival) one week May–Jun in Sarayiçi, 2km from Edirne

EDİRNE ⊙⊙

It is hard to imagine that this sleepy border town, ancient Hadrianopolis, was once the capital of the Ottoman Empire. In its centre is the town's oldest mosque, the nine-domed Eski Cami. Next to it is the beautifully restored Rüstem Paşa Caravanserai, the Bedesten, Edirne's first covered market, and further on the Semiz Ali Paşa Çarşısı, built by Sinan in 1560 but now closed because of a fire. The nearby Üç Şerefeli Camii (Mosque of Three Balconies), built by Murat II in 1447, was the first grand Ottoman mosque, with a sweeping central dome and tall, slender minarets. A few hundred metres away stands the astounding Selimiye Camii, built by Mimar Sinan for Selim II in 1575. It dominates Edirne. The master architect considered the mosque to be his finest work, an architectural feat completed at the age of 80. It is now regarded as the culmination of classical Ottoman architecture. The grand dome is slightly larger than at the Aya Sofya, sunlight flows through stained-glass windows, and the white marble, calligraphic decoration and early İznik tiles together give an immediate sense of perfect harmony. Its 70m-high minarets are amongst the world's tallest. The *medrese* (Islamic school) houses the Museum of Turkish and Islamic Arts, which has an interesting gallery of portraits of the local wrestling champions. The 15th-century Muradiye Camii, on the edge of town, is decorated with marvellous İznik tiles. Several historic bridges cross the River Tunca, but the riverbanks are a military zone.

İZNİK ✪✪

Between the 15th and 17th centuries, İznik, ancient Nicaea, produced some of the most beautiful faience tiles in the Ottoman Empire. Production began after Sultan Çelebi Mehmet I imported craftsmen from Persia. At the peak period, the end of the 16th century, the town had more than 300 working kilns. The ancient defence walls, built around 300 BC, still surround most of the town. They are entered through the double İstanbul Kapısı (Gate). Between the gates stands a triumphal arch that honours Emperor Hadrian. İznik's most important Byzantine monument is the Ayasofya Basilica, built by Justinian in the 6th century, but restored many times since then. Converted into a mosque after the Ottoman conquest, it is now a dilapidated museum displaying some mosaic flooring and a superb fresco. In the northeast quarter of town is the oldest-known Ottoman mosque, Hacı Özbek Camii, built in 1333, and a *medrese*, Süleyman Paşa

➕ 87D1
✉ 85km from Bursa, 230km from İstanbul
🕐 Ayasofya Basilica: daily 9–12, 1–5. Archaeological Museum: Tue–Sun 8:30–12, 1–5:30
🍴 Çamlık on the lake shore (£) its speciality is local catfish (*yayin*)
🚌 Buses from İstanbul Topkapı Otogar (3hr 30) and buses from Bursa (1hr 15)
ℹ Tourist Office at Belediye İşhani Kat:1, no. 130–1
☎ 224-757 19 33
♿ None

Medrese, still used as a Koranic school. The park is home to several monuments, including the 14th-century Yeşil Cami and its green minaret and the interesting Archaeological Museum, housed in the attractive 14th-century Nilüfer Hatun İmareti (Hostel). You can swim in the nearby lake, but the beaches are far from inviting.

The grandest Ottoman monuments were decorated with İznik tiles

KİLYOS ✪✪

Kilyos is a popular holiday resort on the Black Sea, overlooked by a medieval Genoese castle (occupied by the military). Its vast stretch of sandy beach is spotlessly clean and in summer is equipped with deck chairs and umbrellas. On summer weekends, when half of İstanbul descends, the beach gets really crowded.

➕ 87C2
✉ 45km from İstanbul on the Black Sea
🍴 Beach restaurants (£–££)
🚐 Minibus marked Kilyos from Sarıyer (► 90)
♿ Few

✚ 82B5

✉ 18km from Istanbul centre, on the European shore of the Bosphorus

🍴 Deniz, fishing harbour (£)

🚌 Dolmuş and minibus from Beşiktaş

🚢 Ferries from Eminönü

♿ None

↔ Sadberk Hanım Müzesi (► 66)

SARIYER

Sarıyer is the largest village on the European shore of the upper Bosphorus, and the busiest fishing harbour on the strait. The pleasant town has several old wooden mansions on the waterfront, but its main attractions are the fishing harbour and the fish market, which are particularly lively when boats return with their catch. Fish restaurants on the front are worth trying out, especially in summer, when the quay becomes an open-air restaurant. The tomb of Tellibaba, near Sarıyer, attracts young girls, who cut a silver thread above the saint's tomb in the hope of finding a husband.

✚ 87D2

✉ 70km from Üsküdar, on Black Sea, Asian shore

🍴 İyot (££), Liman Yolu (private beach near port)

🚌 Buses from the western bus station at Üsküdar

♿ None

The popular resort of Şile

ŞİLE

Şile is a rather ordinary resort, but the closest to Istanbul. On summer weekends it suffers for its proximity and the beaches are packed. On other days, when you can still see the white sandy beaches, the bay looks quite attractive, with a black and white lighthouse and the ruins of a 14th-century Genoese castle on a nearby island. The quiet neighbouring fishing village of Ağva is scenically located between two rivers. Boats go to the often deserted Karabatak Beach.

✚ 87D1

✉ 257km from Istanbul, 24km from Bursa

🍴 Sarıalan (££–£££)

🚌 Dolmuş marked *Teleferik* from Atatürk Cad., Bursa; then cable car (*teleferik*) to Sarıalan

ULUDAĞ (GREAT MOUNTAIN)

At 2,543m, Mount Uludağ is Turkey's most popular ski resort, set in a forested national park. Serious skiers and hikers, however, will prefer the area outside the park near Sirk gölleri, which is quieter and more beautiful, and has several lakes near the summit. Spring is a good time to visit, with wild flowers starting to bloom in the milder weather. The skiing season is December–March.

Where To...

Above: *bright and tassled Turkish slippers*
Right: *street vendors sell* simit *bread rings for snacks*

Turkish/Ottoman Restaurants

Turkish Restaurants

Most restaurants in Istanbul are relatively cheap compared to those in Western Europe. Ingredients are usually fresh and the average standard of cooking is high. Five-star hotel restaurants, popular with the Istanbuli wealthy class, are obviously more expensive but often worth the extra. However, you never need go hungry in Istanbul because wherever you go you will find cheap and delicious street food. Price per person for a full-course meal with drinks – superb.

£	= up to £6
££	= £6–15
£££	= over £15

Asitane (£££)

'Nouvelle' Ottoman cuisine accompanied by classical Turkish music (evenings only) with great views over this charming area. Garden terrace in summer.

✉ **Kariye Hotel, Kariye Camii Sokak 18, Edirnekapı** ☎ **534 84 14** 🕐 **Lunch, dinner**

Beyti (£££)

This famous restaurant, established in the 1940s, claims to serve some of the best grills in Europe. The hideous façade hides no less than 5 kitchens, 11 dining rooms, 3 terraces and several Ottoman salons. Presidents and pop stars have eaten here, and everyone agrees that the mixed grill is superb and the *künefe* for dessert is even better.

✉ **Florya, near the airport** ☎ **663 29 90** 🕐 **Lunch, dinner. Closed Mon** 🚃 **Banliyö train from Sirkeci**

Borsa (££)

Not to be confused with the new Borsa fast-food chain, this restaurant serves a wide variety of fine traditional Anatolian dishes that rarely appear on restaurant menus.

✉ **Lütfü Kırdar Kongre ve Sergi Salonu, Harbiye (near the Hilton)** ☎ **232 42 01** 🕐 **Lunch, dinner**

Darüzziyafe (££)

Housed in a side building of the Süleymaniye mosque, Darüzziyafe serves delicious Turkish food at very reasonable prices beneath a superb vaulted ceiling. No alcoholic drinks.

✉ **Şifahane Caddesi 6, near the Süleymaniye Camii** ☎ **511 84 14** 🕐 **Lunch, dinner**

Darüzziyafe II (££)

Excellent Turkish food served in a pleasant terracotta-coloured interior, with good views of the neighbouring Sultanahmet Camii (Blue Mosque). In summer there is a peaceful terrace that has even better views.

✉ **At Meydanı 27, next to Sultanahmet Camii, Sultanahmet** ☎ **518 13 51** 🕐 **Lunch, dinner** 🚃 **Tram stop Sultanahmet**

Develi (££)

Extremely popular with Istanbulis for its Anatolian specialities including a delicious kebab with aubergines and pistachio nuts, and their famous *künefe* dessert. Recommended and great fun. Roof terrace in summer.

✉ **Balıkpazarı, Gümüşyük Sokak 7, Samatya** ☎ **529 08 33** 🕐 **Lunch, dinner**

Galata (££)

Modern version of a Turkish tavern (*meyhane*), where traditional Turkish food comes with a lively atmosphere, lots of drinks and Turkish music.

✉ **İstiklâl Caddesi, Orhan Apaydın Sokak 11, Beyoğlu** ☎ **293 11 39** 🕐 **Evening 6–2. Closed Sun. Live *fasıl* music 9–midnight**

Hacı Abdullah (£)

Much frequented by tourists, Hacı Abdullah serves good Turkish dishes in a charming room. The walls are lined with big, colourful jars of fruits preserved in syrup – a speciality, like their delicious *çömlek* (kebab stewed in a terracotta dish) and *beğendili kebab* (aubergine purée). The desserts are notorious: cream with fresh strawberries or *künefe*. Everybody should eat here at least once.

✉ **Sakizağaci Caddesi 19, off İstiklâl Caddesi** ☎ **293 85 61** 🕒 **Lunch, early dinner (closes at 9:30PM). In Ramazan open only after sunset**

Hacı Baba (£–££)
Another popular place, with a large choice of tasty dishes. Service can be slow. In summer eat out on the lovely terrace overlooking a little Orthodox church. A good place for lunch.

✉ **İstiklâl Caddesi 49, Taksim** ☎ **244 18 86** 🕒 **Lunch, dinner**

Hala (Mantı ve Ev Yemekleri Salonu) (£)
An excellent choice for a cheap dinner or a late afternoon snack. Try the Anatolian speciality of *mantı* (Turkish ravioli stuffed with meat) in yoghurt sauce, or delicious pancakes, prepared by the old women sitting in the window.

✉ **Büyükparmakkapı, Çukurlu Çeşme Sokak 26, Beyoğlu (off İstiklâl Caddesi)** ☎ **293 75 31** 🕒 **7AM–midnight**

Havuzlu (£)
The best restaurant in the Kapalıçarşı (Covered Bazaar) by far, offering a large choice of vegetable and meat dishes, and a welcome rest from shopping.

✉ **Gani Çelebi Sokak PTT Yani 3** ☎ **527 33 46** 🕒 **Lunch only. Closed Sun**

Kanaat Lokantası (£)
Founded in 1933, this famous restaurant serves 150 well-prepared traditional Turkish dishes, all presented on a heated counter. A good place for lunch, when the food is fresher. No alcohol.

✉ **Selmanipak Caddesi 25, near the Üsküdar ferry landing, Üsküdar** ☎ **0216-333 37 91** 🕒 **Lunch, dinner**

Kimene Restaurant (££)
One of the best restaurants in the old flower market, serving good food in a pleasant atmosphere. The music goes on until late, so eat in the upstairs dining room if you want quiet.

✉ **Çicek Pasajı, off İstiklâl Caddesi** ☎ **244 12 66** 🕒 **Lunch, dinner**

Karabiber (£)
This tiny restaurant is run by a foundation that promotes women's labour. It offers delicious, little-known dishes from different regions of Turkey. Everything is strictly natural, and this is as close as you get to home-cooking.

✉ **Asmalı Mescit, General Yazgan Sokak 3, Tünel Beyoğlu** ☎ **251 90 85** 🕒 **9AM–6PM**

Konyalı Topkapı Sarayı Restaurant (£££)
The restaurant in the Topkapı Museum offers a welcome break from the glut of treasures on display in the galleries. Excellent Turkish food and splendid views over the Boğaziçi (Bosphorus) and Marmara Denizi (Sea of Marmara).

✉ **4th courtyard of the Topkapı Sarayı Museum, Sultanahmet** ☎ **513 96 96** 🕒 **Lunch only**

Lokanta III Mevki (£)
Charming tiny restaurant (only five tables), decorated with jars of home-made fruit and vegetable pickles. Run and frequented by young people. The menu changes daily. Recommended.

Tripe Soup or İşkembe Çorbası
After enjoying Istanbul's buzzing nightlife, many Turks like to drink a bowl of *işkembe çorbası* before going to bed. Although it is said to be a most effective hangover cure, you can have it any time of the day. Places selling *işkembe* always stay open until the early morning. Try: Ahmet Rasim ✉ Ebulula Caddesi 27, Levent; Çifte Saraylar ✉ Birinci Caddesi 38, Arnavutköy, or Sarnıç ✉ Teşvikiye Caddesi 46, Teşvikiye.

Something Fishy

Most restaurants have a few fish dishes on the menu but if you are serious about fish or seafood, head for the waterfront somewhere. One of the most famous places to eat fish is in Kumkapı, overlooking the Marmara Denizi (Sea of Marmara) and Adalar (Princes' Islands). The old Byzantine harbourfront is a pedestrian zone, with several restaurants displaying their selection of fresh fish. The best fish restaurants, however, are on the Bosphorus (► 98–9).

✉ Büyük Parmakappi, Gümzü Han 9, off İstiklâl Caddesi, Taksim 🕐 Lunch, dinner

Liman Lokantası (£££)

This was the place to be in the 1950s when it was run by Atatürk's cook Fontana. It has reopened in style, serving excellent Turkish and international delights. To accompany the food there is a fantastic view of the working harbour and the mosque of Sultanahmet in the background.

✉ Rıhtım Caddesi, Yolcu Salonu Üstü K3, Karaköy (above the arrivals hall for passenger ships) 🕾 292 39 92
🕐 Lunch, dinner. Booking essential

Murat (£–££)

Reasonably priced excellent Turkish dishes, particularly the speciality lamb dishes. Friendly service.

✉ Ordu Caddesi 212a, Beyazıt 🕾 528 19 28 🕐 Breakfast, lunch, dinner

Musa Ustam Adana (£)

This kebab salon on three floors is a real institution in the Taksim area. The *meze* are excellent, but the restaurant is especially renowned for its brochettes grilled on a wood fire. The food is delicious, so it is always crowded. Recommended.

✉ Küçükparmakkapı 14 🕾 245 29 32 🕐 All day

Pandeli (££)

Pandeli's food is not as good as it used to be, but the kebab with a yoghurt sauce is still good and the surroundings make it worth braving the slow service. Try to get a table where you are overlooking the market.

✉ 1st floor of Mısır Çarşısı (Egyptian Spice Bazaar), Eminönü 🕾 527 39 09
🕐 Lunch only. Closed Sun

Pera Palas Restaurant (£££)

Magnificent and formal restaurant in this legendary hotel with sumptuous period décor and reasonably priced but often mediocre food. Orchestra in the evenings.

✉ Pera Palas Oteli (► 63)
🕾 251 45 60 🕐 Lunch, dinner

Pudding Shop (£)

This once-famous restaurant has sold its soul and become just another cheap self-service place, with mediocre food, but it still lives on its reputation as the meeting place for travellers en route to India. A general hip hang-out, it's for nostalgics only.

✉ Divan Yolu 6, Sultanahmet 🕾 522 29 70 🕐 All day
🚊 Tram stop Sultanahmet

Rami (££)

Elegant Ottoman-style dining room decorated with the works of the impressionist painter Rami Uluer. The menu covers the usual classic Turkish dishes, and from the windows you can see the illuminated Sultanahmet.

✉ Utangaç Sokak 6, Sultanahmet 🕾 517 65 93
🕐 Daily, breakfast, lunch, tea, dinner

Refik's (£)

Modest Turkish *lokanta* serving specialities from the Black Sea such as stuffed cabbage. Refik Baba, the owner, is quite a character and likes a chat

and a good joke or two.

✉ **Sofyalı Sokak 10–12, Tünel** ☎ **243 28 34** ◷ **Lunch, dinner. Closed Sun**

Rumeli Café (££)

Simple but well-prepared Turkish dishes, served in a rustic interior that feels more like a Parisian bistro. Friendly service and pleasant, chatty owner.

✉ **Divan Yolu, Ticarethane Sokak 8, behind the restaurant Vitamin, Sultanahmet** ☎ **512 00 08** ◷ **Daily, 10AM–2AM** 🚊 **Tram stop Sultanahmet**

Sarnıç (£££)

Sarnıç's atmospheric and stylish restaurant occupies a Byzantine cistern that in recent times was used as a car repair workshop. The excellent food is served by candlelight and with guitar music. Spectacular, if touristy.

✉ **Soğukçeşme Sokağı, Sultanahmet** ☎ **512 42 91** ◷ **Lunch, dinner**

Yeşil Ev Restaurant (££)

Inventive Turkish food and international dishes served to live violin accompaniment in a stylish room. For even better surroundings (in summer) there is the wonderful garden.

✉ **Kabasakal Caddesi 5, between Aya Sofya and Sultanahmet Camii, Sultanahmet** ☎ **517 67 86** ◷ **Breakfast, lunch and dinner** 🚊 **Tram stop Sultanahmet**

Fish & Seafood

Huzur (Arab'in Yeri) (££)

Well-known and popular restaurant serving excellent fish, with spectacular views over the European side of Istanbul.

✉ **Salacak İskelesi 20, Üsküdar** ☎ **0216-333 31 57** ◷ **Lunch, dinner**

Inci (£££)

Vast café-restaurant serving fish specialities in a magnificent location, on the waterfront looking on to Topkapı Sarayı and the Boğaziçi (Bosphorus).

✉ **Salacak Sahil Yolu 1, Üsküdar** ☎ **0216-310 69 98** ◷ **Lunch, dinner**

Kartallar (££)

The friendly owner serves some of the freshest fish in the area, and the quality of the cooking is excellent.

✉ **İstasyon Caddesi 21, Kumkapı** ☎ **517 22 54** ◷ **Lunch, dinner**

Livar (££)

Wonderful seafood and fish restaurant with great views over the nearby Adalar (Princes' Islands).

✉ **İskele Caddesi 25/1, Caddebostan, on the Asian side of the Marmara Denizi (Sea of Marmara)** ☎ **0216-411 17 00** ◷ **Lunch, dinner**

Sale e Pepe (£££)

Pleasant restaurant serving well-prepared Italian seafood dishes – might make a welcome change.

✉ **Ebulula Caddesi 31, Etiler** ☎ **280 88 03** ◷ **Lunch, dinner**

Sea House Restaurant (£££)

One of the best places in town to eat seafood. A wonderful room overlooking the Boğaziçi.

✉ **Muallim Naci Caddesi 133, Kuruçeşme near Ortaköy** ☎ **287 12 77** ◷ **Lunch, dinner**

Restaurant Streets

The old flower market, Çiçek Pasajı, and Balık Pazarı, the Fish Market, off İstiklâl Caddesi, are both lined with authentic and charming little eateries serving *meze*, and seafood dishes. Although tourists have more than discovered the place, it is still popular with locals, who come for a few beers or *rakıs* while listening to gypsy musicians play their accordions and violins. Just off the market is a less touristy street, Nevizade Sokak, whose restaurants have terraces outside in summer.

International Cuisine

Health Food

More and more Istanbulis are taking an interest in health food, and wholefood shops are popping up everywhere. The recently opened Mangia café-restaurant in the upmarket department store Mudo in Nişantaşı (☎ 234 62 20) is typical, serving various fruit and vegetable juice cocktails, as well as sandwiches, American cookies, teas and speciality coffees.

Restaurants

Café du Levant (£££)

The restaurant of the Rahmi M Koç Industrial Museum specialises in good French bistro cuisine prepared by French chefs. Rather unusual surroundings for Istanbul.

✉ KoçMuseum Hasköy Caddesi 27, Sütlüce ☎ 250 89 38 🕒 Lunch, tea, dinner. Closed Mon

Çin Lokantası (££)

By far the best Chinese restaurant in Istanbul, this also has Turkish dishes on its extensive menu. Delightful old-fashioned décor.

✉ Lamartin Caddesi 17/1, Taksim ☎ 250 62 63 🕒 Lunch, dinner

Flamingo (££)

Excellent French food – the steaks are superb – sharp service and live French music in the evenings. Good value.

✉ Receppaşa Caddesi 15/1, Taksim ☎ 250 63 22 🕒 Lunch, dinner

Four Seasons (££)

Run by an English woman and her Turkish husband, this Istanbul institution is popular with the staff of nearby embassies. It serves both Turkish and Mediterranean specialities in elegant surroundings.

✉ İstiklâl Caddesi 509, Beyoğlu ☎ 293 39 41 🕒 Lunch, dinner

Gargantua (£££)

Beautiful French restaurant in the trendy Ortaköy district, inventive French cuisine, friendly service.

✉ Vapur İskelesi Sokak 5, Ortaköy ☎ 259 17 86/89 🕒 Mon–Sat lunch, dinner

Kathisma (££)

Simple but delicious Mediterranean cuisine, including good Turkish dishes, served in a converted house with wooden floors and bare brick walls. Excellent chicken with thyme, courgette fritters and stuffed figs.

✉ Yeni Akbıyık Caddesi 26, Cankurtaran ☎ 518 97 10 🕒 Lunch, dinner

Nature and Peace (££)

Deliciously prepared health food, which is cooked to order. There can be a bit of a wait, but it is worth it.

✉ İstiklâl Caddesi, Büyükparmakkapı Sokak 21, Beyoğlu ☎ 252 86 09 🕒 Lunch, tea, dinner

Park Şamdan (£££)

A consistent favourite of well-heeled Istanbulis, with some of the best food and slickest waiters in town. Definitely a place to go if you want to see and be seen, but be sure to dress up.

✉ Mim Kemal Öke Caddesi 18/1, Nişantaşı ☎ 225 07 10 🕒 Lunch, dinner. Closed Sun lunch

Pars (££)

The only Persian restaurant in town, in a lovely old house, serving authentic Persian cuisine in a very relaxing atmosphere.

✉ Meşrutiyet Caddesi 187, Tepebaşı ☎ 292 18 46 🕒 Breakfast, lunch, tea, dinner

Rejans (££)

Formerly considered the smartest restaurant in town, Rejans is now a slightly shabby Russian restaurant, but is still renowned for deadly home-made lemon vodka and extremely surly waiters.

Atatürk loved it. Booking for dinner is essential.

✉ **Emir Nevruz Sokak 17, Galatasaray** ☎ **244 16 10**
🕐 **Lunch, dinner. Closed Sun**

Ristorante Rosa (£–££)

A pleasant Italian restaurant currently serving some of the best pizzas in town.

✉ **Cumhuriyet Caddesi 131, next to the Hilton Hotel, Taksim**
☎ **241 28 27** 🕐 **Lunch, dinner**

Seasons (£££)

As well as its Turkish menu, the trendy Seasons also serves an international menu that combines the best of French and Italian cuisine with a flavour of the Far East. Recommended, but you might need to book.

✉ **Four Seasons Hotel (Hotels, ➤ 100)**

Sepetçiler Kasrı (£££)

Wonderful building in the Sepetçiler Pavilion serving good international cuisine, with superb views of the Bosphorus. Book ahead.

✉ **Kennedy Caddesi, Sarayburnu** ☎ **514 06 73**
🕐 **Lunch, dinner**

Patisseries

Hacı Bekir (£)

By far the best *lokum* in town and excellent Turkish pastries. (Shopping, ➤ 109)

✉ **Hamidiye Caddesi 83, Eminönü (and İstiklâl Caddesi, next to Vakko)** 🕐 **All day**

Hacıbozan (£)

The sweetest and most delicious Turkish pastries are served with a glass of *ayran* (salted yoghurt drink).

✉ **Ordu Caddesi 279, opposite Laleli Camii** ☎ **518 92 24**
🕐 **All day**

İnci Pastanesi (£)

There is rarely a place to sit in this tiny patisserie, popular with Istanbulis, who come for the profiteroles dripping in chocolate sauce. İnci claims they invented the recipe, but we have eaten better.

✉ **İstiklâl Caddesi 122–124, Beyoğlu** ☎ **243 24 12**
🕐 **All day**

Koska (£)

This restaurant serves delicious pastries and Turkish delights. It is very popular with the students from Beyazıt University across the road.

✉ **Yeniçeriler Caddesi 81**
🕐 **All day**

Cafés

Fes Café (£)

Excellent coffee, both Turkish and a good caffe latte. Run by friendly young guys, who also sell delicious home-made cakes.

✉ **Halıcılar Caddesi (Carpet Sellers' Bazaar) 62, Kapalıçarşı**
☎ **527 36 84** 🕐 **Mon–Sat 9:30–7**

Gila Istanbul Sanatıarı Çarşı (£)

A peaceful tea garden with views of the minarets and domes of the Aya Sofya and Sultanahmet mosque.

✉ **In the old *medrese* next door to the Yeşil Ev Hotel (Hotels, ➤ 101)** 🕐 **All day**

Piyer Loti Café (£)

Favourite haunt of the French writer Pierre Loti (➤ 14). Magnificent views of the Haliç (Golden Horn), and tables in the garden.

✉ **15 minutes' walk from the Eyüp Camii** ☎ **581 26 96**
🕐 **Daily 10–10**

Aşure or Noah's Pudding

Aşure is now available in sweet shops and restaurants for most of the year, but it was originally a food prepared to break the Ramazan fast. It is supposed to be made with 40 ingredients, as legend has it that when Noah saw land after his 40-day sail, he gathered up the remaining supplies on board (there happened to be 40 ingredients), and made a stew of them. Today you can buy a packet of pre-mixed *aşure* in markets, but the number of ingredients seems to have diminished dramatically.

Outside Istanbul City Centre

A Turkish Meal

There's little chance of going home hungry when you eat *alaturca*. Traditionally the meal starts with a selection of *soğuk meze,* or cold starters, followed or accompanied by a plate of *sıcak meze* or hot hors d'oeuvres. The main course is always simple, often grilled meat, kebab or fish, served with bread and salad. Baked pumpkin or quince with clotted cream and nuts, rice pudding, fruit preserves or fruit (*meyve*) are popular desserts (*tatlı*). The meal ends with a strong digestive Turkish coffee (*kahve*).

Adalar (Princes' Islands)

Kaptan Lokantası (££)
Overlooking the harbour and sea, the Kaptan is a bit of an institution on the island, with friendly service and excellent fish. The speciality is turbot.

✉ **Liman Çıkmazı Sokak 11A, Büyükada** ☎ **0216-382 34 16**
🕐 **Lunch, dinner (often closed in winter)**

Yörük Ali Restaurant (£)
Simple, brightly painted restaurant with beach and sea view, offering basic Turkish and international dishes.

✉ **Follow the coast road to the right of the ferry landing to the small resort on the headland** ☎ **0216-382 74 54** 🕐 **Lunch, dinner (in summer only)**

Boğaziçi (Bosphorus)/Sarıyer

Deniz (£–££)
Tiny restaurant, which spills on to an outdoor terrace in summer, serving fried sardines and red mullet, squid and shrimps with bread and salad. Very friendly service.

✉ **Fishing harbour in Sarıyer**
🕐 **Lunch, dinner**

Denizkızı Balık Lokantası (££)
A large, no-nonsense fish restaurant, on the shores of Büyükçekmece, where they serve up just about everything that swims. Excellent quality and quick service.

✉ **İskele Caddesi Liman Sokak 1, Mimarsinan-Büyükçekmece** ☎ **883 36 26**
🕐 **Lunch, dinner**

Kıyı (£££)
Atmospheric fish restaurant, excellent service, delicious fish and seafood. The walls are decorated with original work by famous Turkish photographers and artists.

✉ **Kefeliköy Caddesi 126, Tarabya** ☎ **262 00 02**
🕐 **Lunch, dinner**

Körfez (£££)
Smart fish restaurant on the waterside. Specialises in sea bass cooked in sea salt. A boat will take visitors across from Rumeli Hisarı by appointment. Book ahead.

✉ **Körfez Caddesi 78, Kanlıca (Asian side of the Bosphorus)** ☎ **0216-413 43 14** 🕐 **Lunch, dinner. Closed Mon**

Marina Restaurant (££)
Charming fish restaurant in an old boat station, serving excellent fish *börek*, shrimp croquettes and fish *meze*. Recommended, especially in summer.

✉ **Kuruçeşme Parkıiçi, Eski Vapur İskelesi, European shore of the lower Bosphorus** ☎ **287 26 53** 🕐 **Lunch, dinner**

Mia Mensa (££)
Excellent Italian restaurant, popular with ex-pat community, overlooking the Bebek dock and Bosphorus.

✉ **Manolya Sokak 244/1, Bebek, European shore** ☎ **263 60 80** 🕐 **Lunch, dinner. Closed Sun.**

Paysage (£££)
Upmarket restaurant for well-heeled, dressed-up Istanbulis. Good fish specialities and prime views of the Bosphorus.

✉ **Hekimler Sitesi, Kanlıca, Asian shore, the hillside road to Hidiv Kasrı** ☎ **0216-322 70 60**
🕐 **Lunch, dinner**

Le Pêcheur (£££)

Excellent fish restaurant on the seafront, with Turkish as well as international fish specialities.

✉ **Yeniköy Caddesi 80, Tarabya** ☎ **262 70 70** 🕔 **Lunch, dinner**

Sirene (£££)

The general consensus is that the Sirene, on the seafront, is the best restaurant in Istanbul for seafood and fish. The house speciality is *balık kavurma*, a baked fish that just tastes out of this world.

✉ **Mezarburnu Caddesi 2, Sarıyer, European shore** ☎ **242 26 21** 🕔 **Lunch, dinner**

Bursa

Arap Şükrü (££)

A very good fish restaurant in a pedestrian street lined with restaurants, open air cafés, and street stalls selling delicious stuffed mussels (*midye*).

✉ **Kuruçeşme Mah. Sakarya Caddesi 6** ☎ **221 14 53** 🕔 **Lunch, dinner**

Cumurcul (££)

The food is rather mediocre but the place itself is worth a visit for its high, painted ceiling, massive crystal chandeliers, sumptuous velvet curtains and grand atmosphere.

✉ **Çekirge Caddesi, at the edge of the Kültür Park** ☎ **235 37 07** 🕔 **Lunch, dinner**

Hünkar Lokantası (£)

Hünkar is locally known for its excellent bread and *pide* (pizzas), which are served with the house speciality of *köfte* (meat balls) and *kebabs*.

✉ **Atatürk Caddesi 90, opposite the post office** 🕔 **Lunch, dinner**

İskender (£–££)

If you eat only one *döner kebab* let it be here where the dish was invented. The restaurant uses meat from sheep that have grazed on aromatic herbs growing on the slopes of Mount Olympus in Uludağ. The excellent food is served in a beautiful dining room of painted wood and stained glass.

✉ **Ünlü Caddesi 7, near the Atatürk statue (Heykel)** ☎ **221 46 15** 🕔 **Lunch, dinner**

Villa Mangal (££)

Delightful restaurant in the mountains, with a tree-shaded terrace. It's the sort of place where you have to barbecue the excellent *pirzolas* (or lamb chops) yourself.

✉ **10km from Bursa on the road to Uludağ (Uludağ Caddesi)** 🕔 **Lunch, dinner**

Edirne

Aile Lokantası (£–££)

Well-established and one of the best restaurants in town, with good Turkish food and neat décor.

✉ **Saraçlar Caddesi, opposite the post office** 🕔 **Lunch, dinner. Closed Sun**

Restaurant of the Kervansaray Oteli (££–£££)

Excellent food, both Turkish and international, served in the wonderful décor of this Sinan-designed caravanserai.

✉ **Eski Cami Yanı (► 103)** ☎ **225 21 95** 🕔 **Lunch, dinner**

İznik

Kırıkçatal Lokantası (££)

Very good but simple fish restaurant in a quiet spot near İznik Gölü (Lake İznik).

✉ **Göl Kiyisi** ☎ **0224-757 11 52** 🕔 **Lunch, dinner**

İskender Kebab from Bursa

The *döner kebab*, a popular dish all over the world, is also known in Bursa as *İskender kebab*. In 1867, Mr İskender, from Bursa, was the first to roast lamb's meat on a vertical spit. The raw lamb's meat is sliced thinly and piled on a long spit which turns in front of a grill. This version is traditionally served as a main course with bread, a little butter, tomato sauce and yoghurt.

In Istanbul

Where to Stay
Most of Istanbul's interesting sights are in the Sultanahmet district, but many of the better hotels were until recently in the Galata/Taksim area. However, with the heavy traffic between those two parts of town and the opening of some excellent hotels in Sultanahmet, it now makes perfect sense to stay near the Aya Sofya. To get away from it all, try one of the hotels on the Boğaziçi (Bosphorus) or Adalar (Princes' Islands).

Sultanahmet area
Armada (£££)
Close to the major sights, this modern hotel has elegant rooms decorated in traditional style. The hotel uses eco-friendly products and has a pleasant Turkish restaurant.

✉ **Ahırkapı Sokak, Ahırkapı** ☎ **638 13 70, fax 518 50 60**

Ayasofya Pansiyonları (£££)
A neat row of old Istanbul houses between the Aya Sofya and the Topkapı Sarıyer walls, painstakingly rebuilt and restored by the Turkish Touring and Automobile Association. The nine houses offer comfort, character and homeliness.

✉ **Soğukçeşme Sokağı, behind the Aya Sofya** ☎ **513 36 60, fax 513 36 69** 🚋 **Tram stop Sultanahmet**

Barut's Guesthouse (£)
Simple, clean and spacious rooms; view of the Bosphorus from the top floor dining room. Friendly service.

✉ **İshakpaşa Caddesi 8, Sultanahmet** ☎ **517 68 41, fax 516 29 44**

Empress Zoe (££)
Stylishly decorated with local furniture and wooden floors. Breakfast and drinks are served on a terrace overlooking the Blue Mosque, the sea walls and the Sea of Marmara. Lovely atmosphere and friendly service.

✉ **Akbıyık Caddesi, Adliye Sokak 10, Sultanahmet** ☎ **518 25 04, fax 518 56 99**

Four Seasons Istanbul (£££)
In the heart of Istanbul's historic quarter, this former political prison has been converted to a luxurious, 65-room palace. Sumptuous rooms are set around a peaceful courtyard filled with plants and birdsong. The interior was decorated by a young Turkish architect who used locally made furniture and age-old painting techniques in a modern way. Friendly and perfect service. Highly recommended.

✉ **Tevkifhane Sokak 1, Sultanahmet** ☎ **638 82 00, fax 638 82 10**

İbrahim Paşa (££)
Hidden away in a corner of the Hippodrome, an old house has been tastefully restored to make this lovely small hotel. Rooms are quite small, but have clean private bathrooms and are decorated with old kilims and photographs. The terrace has a panoramic view of the Sea of Marmara and Sultanahmet, particularly beautiful at sunset.

✉ **Terzihane Sokak 5, Sultanahmet** ☎ **518 03 94, fax 518 44 57**

Kariye (££)
Charming hotel, away from the Sultanahmet area next to the Kariye Camii, built in the style of an old wooden mansion. Rooms are decorated in Ottoman style and equipped with all mod cons; some have excellent views over the city. Very good restaurant Asitane (► 92).

✉ **Kariye Camii Sokağı 18, Edirnekapı** ☎ **534 84 14, fax 521 66 31**

Konuk Evi (£££)
Another creation of the Turkish Touring Club in an old restored mansion with a

large tree-shaded garden overlooking the neighbourhood. The restaurant is in a conservatory and the lobby is furnished with antiques.

⊠ Soğukçeşme Sokağı
☎ 514 02 16, fax 514 02 13

Kybele (££)
Comfortable and charming hotel in the heart of Sultanahmet with pleasant rooms and colourful communal areas decorated with hundreds of coloured lights.

⊠ Yerebatan Caddesi 33–35
☎ 511 77 67; fax 513 43 93
🚊 Tram stop Sultanahmet

Park (£)
Clean rooms with or without private bathrooms. There is an exceptional view from some of the rooms and from the terrace over Sultanahmet and the Sea of Marmara.

⊠ Utangaç Sokak 26 ☎ 517 65 96, fax 518 96 02

Pension Side (£)
Well-kept pension run by an Istanbuli and his Canadian wife, with spotless rooms with or without private showers. Breakfast is served on a terrace.

⊠ Utangaç Sokak 20 ☎ 517 65 90, fax 517 65 90

Poem (£–££)
Rooms in this tiny hotel have poems on the door instead of numbers. Most overlook the sea, some a courtyard with trees. Friendly service, excellent breakfast.

⊠ Akbıyık Caddesi, Terbıyık Sokak 12 ☎ 517 68 36, fax 529 38 07

Şebnem Hotel (£)
Run by a painter of Ottoman miniatures, this small but atmospheric hotel is located near all the sights yet in a quiet back street. A good breakfast is served on the terrace, with a fine view.

⊠ Akbıyık Caddesi, Adliye Sokak 1 ☎ 517 66 23, fax 638 10 56

Sokullu Paşa (££–£££)
Wooden house with very pleasant and comfortable rooms, some of which overlook the pretty courtyard, where breakfast is usually served. The hotel has its own Turkish bath, and remnants of Byzantine walls are visible in the basement.

⊠ Küçükayasofya Mahşehit Mehmetpaşa Sokak 5/7 ☎ 518 17 90, fax 518 17 93

Yeşil Ev (£££)
The 'green mansion', once home to a minister, was carefully rebuilt by the Turkish Touring and Automobile Association and furnished in the style of a 19th-century winter mansion. Excellent, peaceful location in the heart of Sultanahmet, with stunning views of the Sultanahmet Camii and Aya Sofya. Highly recommended.

⊠ Kabasakal Caddesi 5
☎ 517 67 86, fax 517 67 80
🚊 Tram stop Sultanahmet

Yüselt Interyouth Hostel (£)
Popular youth hostel with clean dormitories, triple and double rooms. Discounts for IYHF, GO25 and ISIC card holders. Cafeteria with garden and (sometimes) live music; laundry service and book exchange.

⊠ Caferiye Sokak 6, beside the Aya Sofya ☎ 513 61 50, fax 512 76 28 🚊 Tram stop Sultanahmet

Hotel Prices
Prices are for double rooms including taxes. They are as follows:

£	= up to £40
££	= £40–£100
£££	= over £100

Hidiv Kasrı

The Hidiv Kasrı (£££) in Çubuklu (☎ 0216-425 06 03), on the Asian shore of the Boğaziçi (Bosphorus), is a grand turn-of-the-century villa built for the last Khedive of Egypt and renovated by the Turkish Touring and Automobile Association, who converted it into a particularly attractive hotel with a commodity rare in Istanbul: absolute quiet. The house is set in a delightful garden and has spectacular views of the Bosphorus. Unfortunately, at the time of writing the hotel section is closed but the restaurant is operating.

Beyoğlu/Taksim

Avrupa (£)

One of the most pleasant low-budget hotels in the area, with simple but clean rooms and good service. Breakfast included in the room rate.

✉ **Topçu Caddesi 32, Taksim**
☎ **250 94 20**

Büyük Londra Oteli (££)

Grand hotel designed by an Italian architect in 1850 in the 'Orient Express' style, with some elegant caryatids greeting you at the entrance. The décor has seen better days and new plumbing would be welcome, but nostalgics will be happy here. From the hotel's top floors there are some great views over Istanbul and the sea.

✉ **Meşrutiyet Caddesi 117, near the Pera Palas in Tepebaşı**
☎ **249 10 25, fax 245 06 71**

Çırağan Palace Kempinski (£££)

A modern hotel annexed to a splendid, restored 19th-century palace where John Kennedy Jr honeymooned. Some rooms overlook Yıldız Parkı, but those on the Bosphorus side are preferable. Even better than these, and also more expensive, are rooms in the older palace.

✉ **Çırağan Caddesi, Beşiktaş**
☎ **258 33 77, fax 259 66 86**

Golden Age I (£££)

This is a 112-room hotel in the heart of the Taksim Elmadağ district. Modern and fully equipped, it has its own health centre and jacuzzi.

✉ **Topçu Caddesi 22, Taksim**
☎ **254 49 06**

Hilton (£££)

When it opened in 1955 the Hilton was the first modern hotel in all of Turkey. In the heart of the business centre, near Taksim and a short walk from the Dolmabahçe Sarayı, it offers comfortable rooms with splendid views of the Bosphorus and the Asian side of the city. It is still a favourite with well-established Istanbuli families, who come to take a good afternoon tea while enjoying the gypsy music or to have dinner on the excellent Bosphorus Terrace. All sports facilities and Turkish bath.

✉ **Cumhuriyet Caddesi 2, Harbiye** ☎ **231 46 50, fax 240 41 65**

Pera Palas Oteli (£££)

Istanbul's legendary hotel opened in 1895 to cater for 'Orient Express' passengers, and now reeking with nostalgia (► 63).

✉ **Off busy İstaklal Caddesi.**
✉ **Meşrutiyet Caddesi 98–100, Tepebaşı** ☎ **251 45 60, fax 251 40 89**

Usta (£–££)

Comfortable rooms, all with bathrooms, air conditioning and satellite television.

✉ **Topçu Caddesi 19, Taksim**
☎ **235 10 00, fax 254 75 95**

Vardar Palace Hotel (££)

Completely restored and refurbished, this hotel was built over a hundred years ago in an eclectic Levantine-Seljuk style. The rooms are equipped with all the mod cons including satellite television.

✉ **Sıraselviler Caddesi 54-56, Taksim** ☎ **252 28 96, fax 252 15 27**

Outside Istanbul City Centre

Adalar (Princes' Islands)

Princess (££)
Pleasant hotel with a good restaurant, casino, swimming pool and discotheque. Spacious rooms overlooking the sea.
 İskele Meydanı 2, Büyükada ☏ 216 382 16 28, fax 216 382 19 49 🕐 Usually closed Oct–May

Splendid Palace (££)
Excellent hotel in a splendid white-domed house, with quiet and comfortable rooms. All mod cons.
✉ Nisan Caddesi 71, Büyükada ☏ 0216-382 69 50, fax 382 67 75 🕐 Closed in winter

Boğaziçi (Bosphorus)

Bebek (££)
Spacious, simply decorated rooms with an excellent view of the Bosphorus in the charming fishing village of Bebek.
✉ Cevdet Paşa Caddesi 113–115, Bebek ☏ 263 30 00, fax 263 26 36

Bosphorus Paşa (£££)
Fourteen luxurious, ornately furnished rooms with jacuzzi, some overlooking the Bosphorus, in a grand *yalı* on the Asian shore of the Bosphorus.
✉ Yalıboyu Caddesi 64, Beylerbeyi ☏ 216 422 00 03, fax 216 422 00 12

Fuat Paşa (££)
Housed in an elegant pink and green Ottoman *yalı*, built in the 18th century, this hotel has comfortable, clean rooms. Large restaurant on the Bosphorus side.
✉ Çayırbaşı Caddesi 238, Büyükdere ☏ 242 98 60, fax 242 95 89

Bursa

Bilgiç (£)
Central but quiet, this hotel offers clean rooms with bathroom. Top floor rooms have a good view.
✉ Başak Caddesi 30 ☏ 0224-220 31 90

Çeşmeli (£)
Quiet hotel near the tourist office, with clean rooms equipped with bathroom and phone. Excellent breakfast buffet.
✉ Gümüşçeken Caddesi 6, Bursa ☏ 0224-15 11

Çelik Palace (££–£££)
Slightly outside the centre, this is the best hotel in Bursa, with very comfortable rooms, a lovely garden and a swimming pool.
✉ Çekirge Caddesi 79 ☏ 0224-233 38 00, fax 0224-236 19 10

Edirne

Efe Hotel (£)
Charming hotel run by young people. The rooms are quiet, bright and spotless, and very good value.
✉ Maarif Caddesi 13, Edirne ☏ 0284-213 61 66, fax 0284-212 94 46

Rüstempaşa Kervansaray Oteli (££)
A 16th-century caravanserai in the heart of Edirne, designed by the architect of the grand Selimiye Mosque, Mimar Sinan. It is a magical place. The 75 rooms are comfortable without being luxurious, each equipped with a period fireplace. Avoid those too close to the discotheque.
✉ Eski Cami Yanı, Edirne ☏ 0284-225 21 95, fax 0284-212 04 62

Budget hotels
In summer the cheaper hotels in Istanbul, particularly in the Sultanahmet area, are full by 10am, so it makes sense to book in advance. The water supply is sometimes cut off throughout the city for most of the day, which makes for very smelly rooms in the heat of the summer. Towels are not provided in cheaper hotels, and breakfast is often *alaturca* which involves olives, tomatoes, cheese, honey and bread washed down with strong tea.

Antiques, Music & Books

Avrupa Pasajı
Those who love little junk shops should check out the beautifully restored Avrupa Pasajı, which runs from the Galatasary Balıkpazarı, or Fish Market (▶ 108–9), to the British Consulate, off İstiklâl Caddesi (▶ 53). Also known as the Passage of Mirrors, it is lined with elegant statues. Here and in the extensive passage running parallel closer to the consulate, are a number of little antique and junk shops selling old postcards and jewellery, or vintage cinema posters.

Antiques

Atrium I
Ali Baba's cave filled with old Turkish ceramics, prints, paintings, Ottoman jewellery and textiles.
✉ Tünel Pasajı 5, 7, Tünel-Beyoğlu ☎ 251 43 02
Also at ✉ Swissôtel Bosphorus shopping arcade in Maçka ☎ 259 01 01 ext 5831

Galeri Alfa
Fine collection of antiques, including rare Ottoman lead soldiers and wonderful antique prints and maps.
✉ Faikpaşa Yokuşu 47/2, Gukurcuma, Beyoğlu
☎ 251 16 72

Hikmet & Pınar
Attractive antiques shop with interesting collection of fine Ottoman weapons, some intricate woodwork and excellent textiles.
✉ Faikpaşa Yokuşu 36, Çukurcuma ☎ 293 05 75

Horhor Bit Pazarı
Interesting flea market spread over five floors; mainly furniture and collectibles from the Ottoman period to today.
✉ Kırık Tulumba Sokak 13/22, Aksaray

İzzet & İpek Günay
This wonderful shop is a must for serious collectors. The upmarket antiques and objets d'art include antique furniture, old Turkish paintings, porcelain and glass.
✉ Abide-i Hürriyet Caddesi, Tayyareci, M Ali Bey Sokak 12, Şişli ☎ 233 07 17

Koleksiyon
Auction house, with excellent old paintings, Ottoman chandeliers, carpets and textiles. Go and look for the pleasure of the eye, as the shop is set up like a huge nomad tent.
✉ Çırağan Sarayı shopping arcade, Çırağan Caddesi 84, Beşiktaş ☎ 236 21 46

Ottomania
Interesting little shop with valuable and rare old maps, engravings and books mainly about Turkey and Constantinople.
✉ Sofyalı Sokak 30-32, Tünel, İstiklâl Caddesi, Beyoğlu
☎ 243 21 57

Sofa Art & Antiques
A fascinating antiques shop selling old prints, maps, books and original Kütahya plates, opaline glass and wonderful textiles. A second branch nearer to the Kapalıçarşı (Covered Bazaar) sells old and new jewellery based on Ottoman originals.
✉ Nuruosmaniye Caddesi 42 and 106b, Cağaloğlu
☎ 527 41 42

Music & Books

Eren
Publisher and bookshop, specialising in Turkish and Islamic studies.
✉ Sofyalı Sokak 34, Tünel, İstiklâl Caddesi, Beyoğlu
☎ 251 28 58

Galeri Kayseri
Good selection of books on Turkish arts and culture, architecture, history and Sufism, as well as guidebooks to Istanbul in several languages. There is also a small collection of miniatures and ceramics.
✉ Divan Yolu 58, Sultanahmet
☎ 512 04 56

Carpets & Kilims, Crafts

Librairie de Pera
One of the oldest and cosiest antiquarian bookshops in town, with a large collection of European, Greek and Arabic books. Very friendly and knowledgeable service.
 Galip Dede Sokak 22, Tünel
☎ 251 19 66

Megavizyon
Very good selection of Turkish pop and rock, as well as hard-to-find Turkish folk and classical music.
✉ **İstiklâl Caddesi 79-8, Beyoğlu** ☎ 293 07 59

Remzi
Foreign-language magazines and newspapers, travel guides, art books and children's books in several languages.
✉ **Rumeli Caddesi 44, Nişantaşı** ☎ 234 54 75

Robinson Crusoe
Excellent bookshop with a good selection of foreign-language books and beautiful art books on Turkey and Islamic architecture.
✉ **İstiklâl Caddesi 389, Beyoğlu** ☎ 293 69 68

Carpets & Kilims

Antikart
The owner is a lover and connoisseur of rare kilims, and has built up a great selection of old and beautiful textiles.
✉ **İstiklâl Caddesi 209, Atlas Kuyumcular Çarşısı, Beyoğlu**
☎ 252 44 82

Şişko Osman Halıcı
Well-known carpet dealers, a favourite of the ex-pat community, with a large selection of old rugs.

✉ **Halıcılar Caddesi 49, Kapalıçarşı, Beyazıt**
☎ 526 17 08
Also at ✉ **Zincirlihan 10-15, Kapalıçarşı**
☎ 526 72 85/6

Maison du Tapis d'Orient
Antique Anatolian and Central Asian carpets and kilims, as well as very fine antique silk embroideries and other textiles.
✉ **Mehmet Çetinkaya, Arasta Bazaar 151, Sultanahmet**
☎ 517 68 08

Crafts

Ev+
Elegant shop with ceramics, glass, textiles and wood made to its own designs.
✉ **Akkavak Sokak 9/3, Nişantaşı** ☎ 232 17 58

Istanbul Handicrafts Centre (El Sanatlari Çarşısı)
Small workshops where traditional crafts are practised and sold. Dolls, ceramics, embroidery and filigree jewellery.
✉ **In the old Cedid Mehmet Efendi Medresesi beside the Yeşil Ev hotel in Kabasakal Caddesi** ☎ 517 67 80

İznik Classics
One of the finest ceramics shops in town, with exquisite copies of 16th-century museum pieces by the famous artist İsmail Yiğit.
✉ **Arasta Çarşısı 67, Sultanahmet** ☎ 517 17 05

Tay
Unusual shop with attractive hand-sculpted candles in all sizes and shapes, including classical statues.
✉ **Topağacı Ihlamur 84a, Teşvikiye** ☎ 289 08 39

Buying a Carpet
Turkish carpets and kilims are still relatively cheap in Istanbul, but beware of the carpet sellers' tricks. Be sure to visit a few shops before buying, and check the enormous variety and prices. Check also if the carpet is colourfast by wetting it with a white cloth. Test to make sure it is wool by burning the edge. Chemical dyes, increasingly used, are brighter than the rarer natural ones. Antique carpets are becoming rare, so get as much information as you can before buying one and don't expect to find a bargain.

Clothes, Jewellery & Leather

The Golden Bazaar

Gold is cheaper in Turkey than elsewhere and is usually 18 or even 22 carat. Traditional jewellery in silver, however, is often expensive as it is sold only in antiques shops. Some of Istanbul's best jewellers are found near the bazaar on Nuruosmaniye Caddesi in Cağaloğlu. Cheaper copies can be found in the Kapalıçarşı, especially in the old Bedesten.

Clothes

The London-based Turkish designer Rifat Özbek is leading the way for many of his young compatriots, and Turkish fashion is booming. Designers often use the finest traditional, local materials such as the famous Bursa silk, fine angora wool, cashmere and the softest leather. Large shopping malls and many new boutiques have recently opened in the upmarket shopping areas of Nişantaşı, Etiler, Şişli and, on the Asian side, in elegant and super trendy Suadiye, particularly on Bağdat Caddesi. More well-known international brands are now also available.

Artisan

Sumptuous clothes, inspired by the rich Ottoman tradition but modern in design. Clothes rails full of raw silks and rich brocades.
✉ Zafer Sokak 5, Nişantaşı
☎ 231 64 33

Beymen

Excellent contemporary Turkish fashion for men and women, with Turkish-made shoes and accessories to match. Worth checking out. International brands are available as well.
✉ Rumeli Caddesi 81, Nişantaşı ☎ 241 12 73

Cotton Bar

Excellent quality cotton men's shirts, both classic and casual style, and good ties.
✉ Teşvikiye Caddesi 168/B Teşvikiye ☎ 232 56 85
Also at ✉ Galleria shopping mall, Ataköy, Rumeli Caddesi 81, Osmanbey

Gönül Paksoy

Exclusive women's fashion, hand sewn in raw silk, linen and wool, as well as a younger, trendy line also made of natural fabrics.
✉ Atiye Sokak, 1–3 and 6a, Teşvikiye ☎ 260 07 37

Neslihan Yargıcı

One of Turkey's leading designers produces stylish fashion for modern Turkish women, often using natural fabrics such as silks and linen.
✉ Kuyulu Bostan Sokak 6, Nişantaşı
Also at ✉ Galleria shopping mall (► 108)

Rekor

Excellent fabric shop with silks, wool and wonderful evening wear materials for those who prefer to have their clothes tailored. Very reasonable prices.
✉ İstiklâl Caddesi 208, Beyoğlu (or afak Sokak 2, Nişantanşı) ☎ 244 26 81

Silk & Cashmere

A favourite of the foreign community, this shop needs little recommendation: exclusive silk and cashmere wear at affordable prices.
✉ Akmerkez shopping mall, Etiler ☎ 282 02 35
Also at ✉ Galleria shopping mall in Ataköy ☎ 559 45 16

Vakko

Istanbul's oldest, and one of its most elegant, fashion houses sells Turkish and imported designer wear; a good fabric department, a wonderful café-patisserie and an art gallery.
✉ İstiklâl Caddesi 123/125, Taksim ☎ 251 40 92
Also at ✉ Akmerkez shopping mall in Etiler ☎ 282 06 95

Vakkorama
A younger, swinging version of the elegant Vakko selling the sort of clothes from which teenage dreams are made.

✉ **Osmanlı Sokak 13, Taksim**
☎ **251 15 71**
Also at ✉ **Rumeli Caddesi 80, Nişantaşı** ☎ **224 40 30**

Jewellery

Gilan
Exclusive jewellery designed in Turkey.

✉ **Çırağan Palace Hotel Kempinski, Beşiktaş**
☎ **236 21 83**
Also at ✉ **Nuruosmaniye Caddesi 58, Cağaloğlu**
☎ **519 30 10**

Hilat
Amazing Ali Baba's cave with exquisite old Ottoman jewellery and genuine Ottoman antiques. Worth the search, though the real thing comes at a price!

✉ **Gallery Şeref Han, 1st floor, Şeref Efendi Sokak 58, off 95/96 Nuruosmaniye Caddesi (coming from Nuruosmaniye Caddesi, turn right before the mosque walls, first street to the right, gallery immediately to the left)**
☎ **512 73 03**

Urart
Turkey's most famous jewellery designer sells silver and gold jewellery and table ware, often inspired by old Anatolian designs.

✉ **Swissôtel Bosphorus arcade, Maçka** ☎ **259 02 21**
Also at ✉ **Abdi İpekçi Caddesi 18/1 Nişantaşı**
☎ **246 71 94**

Venus
This well-established shop sells antique Turkish silver

jewellery and strings of amber at reasonable prices.

✉ **Kalpakçılar Caddesi 160, Covered Bazaar (▶ 20)**

Leather

Angel Leder
One of Istanbul's better leather stores, just outside the Covered Bazaar, this has an excellent selection of well-designed, quality clothes.

✉ **Veşirhan Caddesi 67, off Divan Yolu**

Çantay
Excellent collection of bags, often in unusual and beautiful colours, in a wide range of shapes and sizes.

✉ **Tepecik Yolu 22, Etiler**
☎ **287 21 53**

Derishow
Contemporary well-designed leatherwear for men and women, as well as clothes in natural fabrics.

✉ **Akmerkez Shopping Mall, Etiler and Akkavak Sokak 18a, Nişantaşı** ☎ **282 03 80**

Modello
Young and trendy or more elegant leatherwear, as well as international brands of men's and women's wear.

✉ **Nispetiye Caddesi 2/1, Etiler**
☎ **257 74 65**

Mihitar Nazaryan
In the heart of the old shoe-makers' area, Mr Nazaryan is the only one who still produces handmade bags and footwear. If you have the time, order a pair of his wonderful shoes. Styles range from classic to the most modern.

✉ **Sıraselviler Caddesi 65, Taksim** ☎ **293 71 79**

Shop till you Drop
Turkey's answer to Saks Fifth Avenue or Harrods is the Beymen Mega Store at Akmerkez Shopping Mall (☎ 282 03 80) in Etiler or in Suadiye on the Asian side (☎ 216 435 48 20). This vast emporium sells everything from Beymen clothing and international fashion designers, to cosmetics, stationery, accessories and even furniture. Bored partners can take refuge in the in-house cinema.

107

Stores & Malls, Markets

Spice of Life

One of the cheapest souvenirs from Istanbul is a selection of spices, obviously best bought from the Egyptian Bazaar or Spice Market (► 59). Choose a place where prices are marked. Turkish or Spanish saffron is very cheap but tasteless, so ask for the slightly more expensive but excellent Iranian saffron, which comes sealed. Other spices to look out for: *Acı biber* (hot chili powder); *tatlı biber* (sweet pepper powder); *yaprak biber* (red pepper paste); *sumak* (purple spice) used in salads and with onions, *kimyon* (cumin).

Department Stores & Malls

Akmerkez

A vast, luxurious shopping mall with everything from exclusive Turkish and international designers to restaurants and cinemas.
✉ **Etiler** ☎ **282 01 70**

Capitol

Another grand shopping and entertainment complex with Çarşı department store, cinemas, restaurants and all the well-known Turkish high-street brands.
✉ **Tophanelioğlu Caddesi, Altunizade-Üsküdar** ☎ **0216-391 18 34**

Carousel

The newest shopping mall in town with Turkish designers as well as such names as Mothercare and British Home Stores. Several shops for kids and a playground.
✉ **Bakırköy** ☎ **570 84 34**

Galleria

The first of the modern malls with branches of all the major chains, Turkish and international, as well restaurants, cinemas and ice rink. Open every day.
✉ **Rauf Orbay Caddesi (Bakırköy highway), Ataköy** ☎ **559 95 60**

Mudo City

Another fashionable department store, on eight floors, with everything from international and local fashion names to trendy children's clothes and home furnishings.
✉ **Rumeli Caddesi 58, Nişantaşı** ☎ **231 36 43**
Also at ✉ **Akmerkez Shopping Mall, Etiler** ☎ **282 04 73**

Markets

Almost every street in Istanbul turns into a market at some time of the day but here are some special ones.

Beyazıt Russian Market

With the collapse of the former USSR, many inhabitants turned to Istanbul as the centre of commerce. They sell in Istanbul whatever they can bring from home, so expect to find anything from fake 501 jeans, textiles, caviar and Russian dolls, to screwdrivers, as well as the consumer goods they take back to sell at home.
✉ **Along the walls of Istanbul University from Beyazıt Meydanı to the Süleymaniye Mosque**
🕓 **Sun mornings only**

Beşiktaş Çarşısı

Daily market for fresh produce and fish, with tiny stalls selling snacks of fresh seafood and hot soup.
✉ **Beşiktaş Meydanı**

Cihangir Bit Pazarı (Flea Market)

An interesting mixture of good junk objects as well as excellent genuine antiques. Look out for Leyla Seyhanlı's antique lace shop.
✉ **Çukurcuma Sokak, off İstiklâl Caddesi**

Egyptian Spice Bazaar (Mısır Çarşısı) (► 59)

Galatasaray Balıkpazarı (Fish Market)

One of the best markets in the city: excellent fresh produce, good caviar, sweets, herbs and spices are usually sold at the local rate rather than at the tourist rate

Food, Sweets &
Caviar

charged at the Egyptian bazaar.

✉ off İstiklâl Caddesi

Ortaköy Sunday Market
A small but pleasant market in the streets of Ortaköy, where stalls sell second-hand books, junk and crafts.

✉ near Ortaköy Camii

Sahaflar Çarşısı
Famous second-hand booksellers' market, which dates back to the 18th century, with wonderful little bookshops and some vendors so rude they are almost charming.

✉ between Beyazıt Camii and the Covered Bazaar

🕐 Mon–Sat 9–7. Closed Sun

Food

Asri Turşucu
A colourful shop which since 1938 has been selling the best pickles of just about every fruit and vegetable.

✉ Firuzağa Camii Karşısı, Cihangir ☎ 244 47 24

Bünsa Baharat
No one will call you into this tiny health food shop that sells excellent spices, natural honey, jams, organic sun dried tomatoes and strings of dried aubergines and peppers at fixed prices. Recommended.

✉ In the Fish Market, Galatasaray ☎ 243 62 65

Kurukahveci Mehmet Efendi
Your nose will lead you to this delicious-smelling but tiny coffee shop where there is usually a queue. Their Turkish coffee powder is an İstanbul institution, and it is generally regarded as the best in town.

✉ Tahmis Caddesi 66, at the back of right fork of the Spice Bazaar, Eminönü ☎ 511 42 62

Sweets & Caviar

Ekmekçioğlu
A tiny shop stuffed with spices, dried fruits, caviar and Turkish delights all sold at fixed prices. Friendly service and a larger selection of spices than most.

✉ İstiklâl Caddesi 51, Beyoğlu ☎ 293 90 24

Sevim İşgüder
Selling by far the best marzipan in Istanbul, this is another Istanbul institution.

✉ Cevdet Paşa Caddesi 238, Bebek, European shore of the Bosphorus ☎ 263 5984

Şekerci Hacı Bekir
Their slogan says it all – 'the best taste since 1777' – and without a doubt they sell the most delicious Turkish delight in town. They have a wide variety, including cream *lokum* and mastic *lokum*, as well as very good halva, chocolates and sugared aniseeds.

✉ İstiklâl Caddesi, next to Vakko, Beyoğlu ☎ 244 28 04 Also at ✉ Hamidiye Caddesi 83 Eminönü ☎ 522 06 66

Üç Yıldız
Paradise for a sweet tooth, this place is considered one of the best confectioners in town selling divine halva with pistachios, natural Turkish jams spooned into jars as you watch, candied chestnuts and their own very good *lokum* in all flavours.

✉ In the Balık Pazarı (Fish Market), off İstiklâl Caddesi, Beyoğlu ☎ 293 87 00

Turkish Delights

Baklava (filo pastry stuffed with nuts and syrup), famous throughout the Middle East, was originally a Turkish invention. *Kadın göbegi* or Lady's navel, are lemon-flavoured cakes soaked in syrup, and *dilber dudağı*, or 'Belle lips', is dough fried in syrup. The delicious *künefe* is angel hair stuffed with a creamy cheese. *Lokum*, or Turkish delight, is basically solidified sugar and pectin, flavoured with mint, rose water, mastic or pistachios.

Children's Activities

Practical Points

Family rooms are quite easy to find in all ranges of accommodation, and in the better hotels cots are available. Baby formulas and jars of babyfood are relatively cheap and readily available, as are disposable nappies. Hotel reception desks may be able to help with baby sitting, or you could try the agency Anglo Nannies London (☎ 265 18 78/79). The international chain Toys'R'Us has opened a 3,000sq m toy store in the Carousel shopping mall in Bakırköy (☎ 543 54 19).

Apart from the Tatilya amusement park there is very little in Istanbul that is specifically designed for children. It may be a difficult city for toddlers, but for those old enough to show some interest in the sights it is a wonderful place to explore. The best time to visit with children is during the spring or late summer, as the high summer months can be hot, sticky and over-tiring. If you do come in the summer try to check into a hotel that has a swimming pool or escape from time to time to the Princes' Islands(➤ 84) or the Black Sea beaches(➤ 89). Children are adored by Turks and they will definitely bring you closer to the people. Travelling as a couple without kids, you will constantly be asked when you are going to produce them.

Anadolu Hisarı

The castle (➤ 32) is probably quite dangerous for children to climb up, but there are rowing boats for hire to explore the two rivers known as the 'Sweet Waters of Asia', a favourite picnic ground during the Ottoman period.

Askeri Müzesi

Children will like the performances of the Janissaries and some may even be interested in the armour on display (➤ 33).

Belgrad Ormanı

A good day out for the family, with walks in the forest or, on a hot day, a picnic (➤ 84). It can be combined with lunch in one of the excellent fish restaurants on the European shore of the Bosphorus (restaurants, ➤ 98).

Birds Paradise and Botanical Garden

More than 70 ha of gardens with zebras, gazelles, kangaroos, penguins and exotic birds, as well as tropical plants.

✉ **In Darıca (45km from Istanbul) E-5 highway on the Asian side**

Cruise on the Bosphorus

Children usually love going on boats and cruising from place to place (➤ 83). Visit the impressive Rumeli Hisari castle (➤ 65) or watch the fishermen come in at Sarıyer(➤ 90)

Deniz Müzesi

Interesting museum for young children, especially the gallery of wonderful caiques and rowing boats (➤ 44).

Gülhane Parkı

Largest park in the Sultanahmet area, good for picnics and running around (➤ 51). Avoid the zoo, as the condition of the animals is appalling.

Tatilya, the Republic of Fun

A Turkish variation of Disneyland, this indoor amusement park is the largest in Europe, and hugely popular with Istanbul's pampered youth. Attractions include 12 theme units, roller-coasters, adventure labyrinth, a lake, a simulation cinema, a shopping centre and restaurants.

✉ **18km west of Istanbul Airport (E-5 Motorway), Beylikdüzü ☎ 872 55 30**
🕐 **Tue–Fri 2–10, Sat–Sun 11–11**

Cinema & Theatre

Cinema

The major cinemas show foreign films with Turkish subtitles, but Turkish films are English-subtitled only at the Istanbul International Film Festival (► 116). Smaller cinemas usually show a dubbed version, so ask at the box office if it is *orijinal* (original version) or *Türkçe* (dubbed in Turkish). Provocative material is censored and some films are cut to fit a time slot. Tickets are cheaper than in Western Europe and matinees are even less expensive. Wednesday is a cheap day at all the cinemas. The *Turkish Daily News* on Sunday has a special weekend section with listings of foreign films.

Alkazar Cinema Centre
Wonderful old cinema in a restored art-nouveau building with three screens and a great café bar for drinks.
✉ İstiklâl Caddesi 179, Beyoğlu ☎ 293 24 66

Feriye
Fine cinema on the Bosphorus with a café-restaurant.
✉ Sabancı Cultural Centre, Ortaköy ☎ 236 28 64

Theatre

Music and theatre festivals attract a large number of Western performers, as well as Balkan, Russian, Arab and Persian artists.

Atatürk Cultural Centre (AKM)
The only purpose-built opera house in Istanbul. The modern premises are shared by the State Opera and Ballet, the Symphony Orchestra and the State Theatre Company. In summer the centre also hosts the popular Istanbul Festival – get tickets and programmes here.
✉ Taksim Meydanı
☎ 251 56 00

Aksanat Cultural Centre
A cultural centre in the heart of the city that organises art and sculpture exhibitions and features regular concerts of classical music and jazz. Turkish drama performances take place and films are shown on the large laser-disc screen. Programmes and tickets are available from the centre.
✉ İstiklâl Caddesi, Akbank Building, Beyoğlu ☎ 252 35 00

Cemal Reşit Rey
An excellent, pleasant concert hall, particularly good for chamber music recitals.
✉ Cemal Reşit Rey Concert Hall, Harbiye ☎ 240 50 12

Istanbul Foundation for Culture and Arts
This foundation is responsible for organising the annual international film festival, theatre and music festivals, as well as the two-yearly Art Biennale, in venues all over the city. For programmes and tickets call their office.
☎ 293 31 33

Süreyya
Undoubtedly Istanbul's most beautiful theatre, built in the 19th century, with painted ceilings and individual boxes.
✉ Bahariye Caddesi 29, Kadıköy, Asian side
☎ 0216–336 06 82

Cultural Centres
Most foreign cultural centres sponsor concerts and exhibitions as well as films, so it is worth checking out their programmes.
British Council, Beyoğlu (☎ 252 74 74),
Casa d'Italia, Tepebaşı (☎ 293 98 48),
French Cultural Centre, Taksim (☎ 249 07 76),
German Cultural Centre, Odakule 286, Beyoğlu (☎ 249 20 09),
USIS (US Info Service), Tepebaşı (☎ 251 36 02).

Sports

Sun and Sea
In summer a great way to relax in the sun is to visit one of the beaches near Istanbul. The best are at Kilyos (➤ 89), Şile (➤ 90) on the Asian shore, or the Adalar (Princes' Islands) (➤ 84). On Büyükada you can hire a horse and carriage to get to the beach.

Edirne
Oil Wrestling
The mid-14th-century Ottoman Sultan Süleyman Paşa organised wrestling competitions between his forty companions and it is these that are commemorated in the annual festival at Edirne. About 800 contestants, fully oiled and dressed only in leather trousers, try to get their adversary down on the floor in less than thirty minutes.

🖂 **Island of Sarayici, 2km from the centre of Edirne**

Istanbul
Burhan Felek Spor Sitesi
One of the largest public swimming pools in town. Although cheap it is often crowded.

🖂 **Nuh Kuyusu Caddesi, Bağlarbaşı, near Üsküdar**
🚌 **Minibus from Üsküdar to Kadıköy**

Fishing from Galata Bridge
Fishing is popular all along the Bosphorus, but fishing from Galata Bridge (➤ 50) is an institution: if it is your first time you will not be short of advice.

Hilton Health Club
At a price, visitors can enjoy the lovely outdoor swimming pool with good views of the Bosphorus, or the indoor pool, jacuzzi, sauna, Turkish bath and gym. Also two squash courts and three tennis courts.

🖂 **Cumhuriyet Caddesi 152, Harbiye** ☎ **231 46 50**
🚋 **Tramway to Taksim**

İnönü Stadium
Turkey's top football teams are based in Istanbul and the most important games are played at this stadium. Turks are mad about football, so it should not be difficult to find out when a match is on.

🖂 **Kadırgalar Caddesi, between Taksim and Beşiktaş**

Kemer Country and Golf Club
Well-maintained 9-hole golf course, soon to be upgraded to 18 holes, set in the Belgrade Forest (➤ 84), with an Ottoman aqueduct in the grounds. Players have to be careful not to slice a ball through one of the surrounding *yalıs* or summerhouses.

🖂 **Göktürk Köyü, Kemerburgaz (30km from the centre)** ☎ **239 79 13, fax 239 73 76**

Klassis Golf and Country Club
Further away from the centre, this club has 18- and 9-hole courses conforming to international standards. The club regularly hosts international tournaments. Rates are cheap compared to Europe and the US.

🖂 **Seymen Silivri, 65km from the centre** ☎ **748 46 00, fax 748 46 43**

Park Orman
Find a large swimming pool, good playgrounds, a theatre and fast-food outlets in the Fatih Children's Woods.

🖂 **Fatih Çocuk Ormanı Maslak Caddesi, Fatih** ☎ **223 07 36**

Rollerblading
Young Istanbuli rollerbladers and rollerskaters practise their art under the watchful eye of the prince of pirates, the statue of Barbaros Hayrettin Paşa, better known as Barbarossa.

🖂 **Beşiktaş waterfront**

Turkish Baths

Hamamı, or Turkish baths, are usually found near a mosque, so the ritual ablutions can be performed before prayers, but they are now mostly used as a public bathroom where you can get a proper scrub. Either the baths have separate men's and women's quarters, or women use the baths in the day time and men in the evening. Bring your own soap and shampoo as they may not be available. After paying the fee you will be shown your changing room locker. Men and sometimes women will be provided with a *peştemal,* a sarong to wrap around the waist, and *takunya,* wooden clogs, and a towel. Men usually keep their sarong on, while many women just wear knickers. The *hararet* or hot room is the main room, where you take a seat by a tap, washing and sluicing yourself with the scoop-dishes. The raised platform in the middle, placed over the furnace, is where the often bone-wrecking massages are given. Shaving usually happens in the *soğukluk* or cooling room, between the reception and hot room. The baths dehydrate you so have some tea or juice afterwards. Drinks, rubs and massages are extras that must be paid for afterwards, and it is customary to leave a tip for the masseur.

Cağaloğlu Hamamı
(► 41)

Çemberlitaş/Hamamı
(► 43)

Çinili Hamamı
This beautifully restored double *hamam* built for Hayrettin Paşa (better known as Barbarossa) is definitely one of the nicest and most authentic in town.
🖂 **just off İtfaiye Caddesi, Zeyrek**

Galatasaray Hamamı
This is a wonderful 19th-century bath, retaining all its original splendour, but beware of the heavy-going massages.
🖂 **Turnacıbaşı Sokak 2, off İstiklâl Caddesi, Beyoğlu**
🕓 **7AM–11PM for men, 8AM–9PM for women**

Gedik Paşa Baths
Dating from 1475, these magnificent baths, recently restored, may well be the oldest in the city. The founder, Gedik Ahmet Paşa, was Grand Vizier under Mehmet the Conqueror and commander of the Ottoman fleet. The *hamam* is capped by an impressive dome and flanked by alcoves and cubicles faced with marble. A popular meeting place for the locals, these baths are spacious, with 27 basins in the men's section and 21 in the women's.
➕ **L12** 🖂 **Gedik Paşa Caddesi** 🕓 **Daily 8–8** 🚇 **Çemberlitaş**

Old Turkish Bath
A 350-year-old *hamam* which is tiny but well run by an anglophile Istanbuli. The baths are open to families after 8PM. Unusually, the male masseur treats both men and women, but he claims to be very honorable as he is married and has 43 children.
🖂 **Alayköşkü Caddesi, off Yerebatan Caddesi**

The famous Bursa baths
Hamam connoisseurs will advise you against a *hamam* experience in Istanbul because the baths have either been turned into tourist sites or lost their soul in renovations. Instead, if you are heading for Bursa (► 86), you must try some of the best *hamamı* in the country, which often date back to Roman times. Çekirge, 2km from the centre, dates from the Justinian era (527–565) and is provided with water from hot sources on Mount Uludağ. Çakır Hamamı, Yeni Kaplıca, Eski Kaplıca and Demirtaş Paşa are all excellent baths in the centre.

Music & Bars, Clubs

Gay Istanbul

Although homosexuality is still taboo, there are several gay bars and discos in the Taksim area. Club 14 (Abdülhakhamit Caddesi 14) and, next door, Club 19 and 20 are popular gay bar-discotheques that stay open at least until dawn. Barbahçe (✉ Sıraselviler Caddesi, Soğancı Sokak 7) is a pleasant gay bar in the Bilsak building. 1001 (✉ Siralselviler Caddesi) is a fun transvestite bar-discotheque that also serves food.

Music & Bars

Adi Bar

A crowded bar situated in Sultanahmet with loud 1980s music and a constant flow of beer. You should be aware that in all the bars in this area undercover policemen have been known to pose as dealers.

✉ İncili Çavuş Sokak 8/1, Sultanahmet

Bilsak 5.Kat

A large bar-cum-restaurant popular with Istanbul's intellectuals, with great views from the top floor over the city and a lively atmosphere.

✉ Siralviler Caddesi, Soğanci Sokaka 7, Cihangir ☎ 252 33 85 🕐 Mon–Sat 10AM–2AM, closed on Sun

Café Gulet

A small bar in the heart of Ortaköy spread over two floors, with very loud live Turkish music. Rakı and beer flow all night and you too can end up dancing on the tables. It is especially lively in winter.

✉ At the centre of Ortaköy ☎ 227 20 92

Dedikodulu Meyhane

This typical tavern has a great atmosphere, featuring live Turkish music (*fasil*). There is also a wonderful and varied selection of *meze*.

✉ Nispetiye Caddesi, Yıldız Çiçeği Sokak 2, Etiler ☎ 265 97 13 🕐 Daily, 9PM–1

Desperado

Avant garde bar, painted electric blue, with good music, Turkish *meze* and a large selection of drinks and cocktails.

✉ Tramvay Caddesi 72, Kuruçeşme ☎ 257 93 55

Gila Bar

Situated on the top floor of a building, this pleasant bar has great views over the surrounding area. Charming service.

✉ Şeftali Sokak, Ateş Pasajı, near Yerebatan Sarayı

Hayal Kahvesi

A pleasant and animated bar and a meeting place for Istanbul's liberated youth. Can be very crowded at weekends, when jazz-rock concerts take place after 10PM.

✉ Büyük Parmakkapı Sokak 19, off İstiklâl Caddesi, Taksim ☎ 244 25 58

Kemanci

An extremely popular venue on three floors with a different, live, nightly music on each – one hard rock, one rock and one surprise.

✉ Sıraselviler Caddesi, off Taksim Meydanı ☎ 251 27 23

Lal

Laid-back bar with good Latin music; serves salads, *böreks* and *meze* with the drinks.

✉ Caferağa Mah. Kadife Sokak 19, Kadiköy ☎ 216 346 56 25

NaturalSam Bar

Great bar with rock and blues music during the day, but live Turkish music on most evenings when the place gets absolutely packed.

✉ Serasker Caddesti, Pavlonya Sokak 40, Kadiköy ☎ (216) 444 77 66 🕐 Daily 10AM–4AM

Orient
Superb bar in this 'Orient Express' hotel with a great atmosphere of slightly faded grandeur.

✉ Pera Palas Oteli (➤ 63), Tepebaşı ☎ 251 45 60

Pupa's
The only bar to serve African food. Tuesdays are for spicy African food and African music, while there is good dancing music (calypso, reggae and salsa) at weekends. Reservations recommended.

✉ 1 Cadde 17, Arnavutköy
☎ 265 65 33

Roxy
Seriously popular venue with frequent live performances by foreign and Turkish rock, jazz and pop groups.

✉ Arslan Yatağı Sokak, off Sıraselviler Caddesi, Taksim
☎ 249 48 39

Sherlock Holmes
A very English pub, as the name suggests, with good Italian and English food and of course a large choice of beers and malt whiskys. Popular hang out for ex-pats.

✉ Çalıkuşu Sokak 5, Levent
☎ 281 63 72

Zihni
Good-looking bar with antique furniture and calligraphy on the wall, for a quieter evening out.

✉ Bronz Sokak 1/b, Maçka
☎ 233 9043

Clubs

Club 29
Disco music is the staple here, drawing a mixed, lively crowd. In summer the club looks out on to the water, and you wine and dine at tables shaded by umbrellas and lit by flaming torches.

🔲 Off map at C16 ✉ Winter: Nispetiye Caddesi 29, Etiler. Summer: Çubuklu ☎ Winter: 263 54 11. Summer: (216) 322 38 88

Galata Tower Nightclub
Situated on the eighth floor of one of Istanbul's most famous landmarks. There are great views of the city by night (if you are not watching the belly-dancing show or hitting the disco).

🔲 29D3 ✉ Kuledibi, Tünel
☎ 245 11 60 🚇 Tünel

Memo's
Swinging open-air joint directly on the Bosphorus, with a good mixture of the latest Turkish hits and excellent dance music. Quite expensive and chic.

✉ İskele Yanı, Ortaköy
☎ 260 84 91 🌀 Only in summer

Pacha Beach
Open-air discothèque on the shore of the Bosphorus, where Istanbul's jetsetters meet. Also a cinema and several bars and cafés.

✉ Muallim Naci Caddesi, Kuruçeşme, just past Ortaköy
☎ 259 70 61 🌀 Only in summer

Süleyman Nazif
The young and beautiful who hang out by the Bosphorus in summer spend their glamorous winter nights here, dancing to the latest Anglo-American hits and watching videos on several screens.

✉ Valikonagı Caddesi 39/1, Nişantaşı ☎ 225 22 43

Cabarets
Several cabarets with such alluring names as Maksim, Regine and Mulinruc offer 'cheap' shows with belly dancers and striptease – but you usually end up with a hole in your pocket. The Yeşil (✉ Abdulhakhamit Caddesi 61, Taksim ☎ 254 3509) features live jazz, rock and Latin music in co-operation with one of the better FM radio stations.

What's On When

Ramazan Nights
Ramazan is the month when Muslims abstain from drinking, eating, tobacco and sex, between sunrise and sunset. The firing of a cannon on Taksim at dusk announces the breaking of the fast. Everything closes slightly earlier during Ramazan so people can get home in time to break the fast at dusk (causing heavy traffic everywhere). Near the major mosques, Fatih (► 48) and Sultanahmet (► 23), the nights are animated with puppet plays (Karagöz), food stalls selling Ramazan dishes, and little cafés with live music.

Exact dates of festivals can be obtained from local tourist offices (► 120). Events are listed in the bi-monthly magazine *Istanbul: The Guide* and in the *Turkish Daily News* on Sunday.

January
New Year's Day: public holiday.

April
Istanbul International Film Festival (early Apr): Turkish (subtitled in English) and foreign films are screened in various cinemas, including the Atatürk Cultural Centre (► 111).
Independence Day, Children's Day (23 Apr): public holiday when children can take over the office of famous people, and young people from all over the world are invited.
Tulip Festival (late Apr–beginning May): in Emigran Park.

May
Atatürk's Commemoration; Youth and Sports Day (19 May): public holiday with many parades all over the country.
Istanbul International Theatre Festival (second half of May).
Fatih day (29 May): Commemoration of the capture of Constantinople by Mehmet II.

June/July
International Offshore Races (Jun) Istanbul–Izmir.
Istanbul International Music Festival (mid-Jun–mid-Jul): performances of Turkish and European ballet, music and opera, as well as rock and jazz, in venues all over the city including the Topkapı

Palace (► 24–5), Aya İrini Kilise (► 34) and Rumeli Hisarı (► 65). Tickets and programmes available from early June from the Atatürk Cultural Centre (► 111).
Folklore and Music Festival (Bursa) (mid-Jun to mid-Jul).

August
Zafer Bayramı (Victory Day), (30 Aug): public holiday celebrating the Turkish victory over the Greeks in 1922.

September
Istanbul Arts Fair (mid-Sep): in the Tüyap Exhibition Centre, Sergi Sarayı, Meşrutiyet Caddesi, Tepebaşi.
Yapı Kredı Art Festival featuring international pop, jazz and classical music.

October
Akbank International Jazz festival (early Oct): performances of Turkish and international jazz bands (information ☎ 252 51 67).
Republic Day (29 Oct): displays and fireworks.

November
Istanbul Book Fair (early Nov): in the Sergi Sarayı, Meşrutiyet Caddesi, near the Pera Palas Oteli (► 63).
Annniversary of Atatürk's death (10 Nov): at 9:05AM the entire country stops for a minute's silence; the boats on the Bosphorus and Golden Horn stop mid-stream and blow their foghorns mournfully.
Istanbul Antiques and Decorative Arts Fair (mid-Nov): in the Ahmet Fethi Paga Rooms at the Military Museum Cultural Centre (Askeri Müzesi ► 33).

Practical Matters

Above: *the floral detail of an İznik tiled wall*
Right: *relaxation Turkish-style – smoking a water-pipe*

WHAT YOU NEED

		UK	Germany	USA	Netherlands	Spain
●	Required					
○	Suggested					
▲	Not required					
Passport/National Identity card		●	●	●	●	●
Visa (obtainable upon arrival)		●	▲	●	●	●
Onward or return ticket		▲	▲	▲	▲	▲
Health inoculations		▲	▲	▲	▲	▲
Health documentation (➤ 123, Health)		▲	▲	▲	▲	▲
Travel insurance (for European and Asian side)		○	○	○	○	○
Driving licence (national or better, international)		●	●	●	●	●
Car insurance certificate		●	●	●	●	●
Car registration document		●	●	●	●	●

WHEN TO GO

Istanbul

■ High season
□ Low season

5°C	6°C	7°C	12°C	16°C	21°C	23°C	23°C	20°C	16°C	12°C	8°C
JAN	FEB	MAR	APR	MAY	JUN	JUL	AUG	SEP	OCT	NOV	DEC

🌧 Wet   ☁ Cloud   ☀ Sun   🌦 Sunshine & showers

TOURIST OFFICES

In the UK
Turkish Tourist Office
First Floor
170–3 Piccadilly
London W1V 9DD
☎ 0171-629 7771
email:
eb25@cityscape.co.uk

In the USA
Turkish Tourist Office
821, United Nations Plaza
New York, NY 100017
☎ 212/687 2194-95
http://www.turkey.org/
turkey

Turkish Tourist Office
1717 Massachusetts
Avenue NW, Suite 306
Washington DC 20036
☎ 202/429 98 44

ARRIVING

The national airline, Turkish Airlines (THY)
(☎ 0171-499 92 49), has scheduled flights from
Britain, mainland Europe and the United States to the
International Terminal of Atatürk Airport in Istanbul
(☎ 663 63 00).

Atatürk Airport Kilometres to city centre	Journey times	
	🚋	N/A
	🚌	1 hour to Askaray
21 kilometres	🚗	30 minutes

Grand Sirkeci (rail) Kilometres to city centre	Journey times	
	🚋	N/A
	🚌	N/A
3 kilometres	🚗	15 minutes

MONEY

The monetary unit of Turkey is the Turkish Lira (TL).
The coinage is 5,000, 10,000, 25,000 and 50,000 lira
pieces. Bank notes are of 50,000, 100,000, 250,000,
500,000 and 1,000,000 and 5,000,000 lira. With inflation
of 100–150% per year, the exchange rates change
daily so it is advisable not to change too much in one
go. You can change money at banks (► 120, Opening
hours) and foreign exchange offices (Döviz Bürosu) at
the airport and all over town (some open until
midnight). Major credit cards can be used to get cash
advances from banks displaying the appropriate sign;
Yapı Kredi, Pamukbank and other ATMs accept Cirrus
and Plus debit cards.

TIME

 Turkey is two hours
ahead of GMT, and
operates a
summertime from late March
to late October when clocks
are put forward one hour.

CUSTOMS

 YES

**Goods Obtained Duty Free
taken into Turkey**
(Limits):
Wine or spirits: 5 x 100ml
Cigarettes: 200
Cigars: 50
Chocolate: 1kg; sweets: 1kg
Coffee:1.5kg
Instant coffee: 1.5kg
Tea: 500gm
Tobacco: 200gm
Perfume: 5 bottles (each
120ml max)
Toilet water: no limit

You are also officially
allowed to take one camera
with 5 rolls of film, one video
camera with 5 blank video
cassettes, one portable
typewriter and one portable
radio when you enter the
country.

 NO

Strictly no narcotics or
weapons. When leaving you
will need to show proof of
purchase for a new carpet or
a certificate from a museum
directorate for old carpets.
Export of antiquities is
forbidden.

TOURIST OFFICES

Head Office
- Meşrutiyet Caddesi 57/5, Tepebaşı, Beyoğlu
  ☎ 243 37 31/243 29 28
  fax: 252 43 46

Branches
- Hilton Hotel, Cumhuriyet Caddesi, Taksim
  ☎ 233 05 92
  🕐 Mon–Sat 9–5

- Taksim Meydanı, next to the French Consulate on İstiklâl Caddesi
  ☎ 245 68 76
  🕐 (only in summer) daily 8:30–12, 1:30–5:30

- Karaköy Limanı Yolcu Salonu (Maritime Terminal), Karaköy
  ☎ 249 57 76

- Sultanahmet Meydanı/ Divan Yolu Caddesi 3
  ☎ 518 18 02
  🕐 daily 8:30–12:30, 1:30–5:30

- Sirkeci Train Station, Sirkeci, Eminönü
  ☎ 511 58 88

- Atatürk Airport, Yeşilköy
  ☎ 663 07 93

NATIONAL HOLIDAYS (► 116)

J	F	M	A	M	J	J	A	S	O	N	D
1			1	2			1		1		

1 Jan   New Year's Day
23 Apr   National Independence and Children's Day
19 May   Atatürk Commemoration and Youth and Sports Day
29 May   Festival commemorating the capture of Istanbul by Mehmet II in 1453
30 Aug   Victory Day
29 Oct   Republic Day
Banks, offices and some shops close on these days.

Religious holidays Most important are the celebration of the end of the Ramazan month of fasting(► 116), the Şeker Bayramı, and the Kurban Bayramı, commemorating Abraham's sacrificing of a sheep instead of his son Isaac. The first lasts three days and the second for four. Both are set by the lunar calendar.

OPENING HOURS

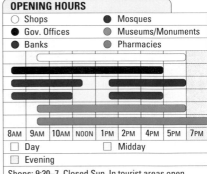

Shops: 9:30–7. Closed Sun. In tourist areas open longer and on Sun.
Covered Bazaar: 8–7. Closed Sun
Government Offices: Mon–Fri 8–4.
Banks: Mon–Fri 8:30 or 9–12, 1:30–5. Longer in tourist areas.
Mosques: bigger mosques dawn to dusk, smaller only at prayer times, five times a day.
Museums: usually 9:30–5 or 5:30. In winter may close 12:30–1:30. Most close Mon and/or Thu.
Pharmacies: 9:30–7, but several all-night chemists.

PUBLIC TRANSPORT

 Internal Flights Turkish Airlines (THY) operate between Atatürk Airport (Domestic Terminal) in Istanbul and all major cities in Turkey. Flights are frequent and quite good value. Main THY office in Istanbul ☎ 248 26 31.

 Trains Istanbul has two railway stations. Grand Sirkeci station in Eminönü is the terminal for European trains(☎ 527 00 50); Haydarpaşa station on the Asian side receives trains from Asian Turkey, Russia and the Middle East (☎ 0216-336 04 75).

 Urban Transport Buses are cheap but uncomfortable; even Istanbulis find it hard to work out which to take. Main terminals are at Topakapı (European side) (☎ 582 1010) and Haren (Asian shore) (☎ 216-333 3763). Minibuses, handy for the trip on the upper road leading to the upper Bosphorus, can be flagged down. The main tramway line runs from Eminönu and Sirkeci station via Ayasofya, Sultanhmet and Beyazıt to Aksaray and Topkapi bus station. An old-fashioned tram runs from Tünel to Taksim along İstaklâl Caddesi. Another line links Aksaray and the bus station (*otogar*), and will soon extend to the airport. One of Europe's first metros (Tünel), links Galata Bridge with İstaklâl Caddesi. Dolmus, collective taxis, are an institution. They drive a fixed route, marked on the window, leaving when full.

 Ferries (*Vapur*) The most efficient and quickest mode of public transport. Ferries travel between the shores of the Golden Horn and the Bosphorus as well as to the Princes' Islands. Boats leave from Eminönü two or three times a day to make the 1½ hour trip up the Bosphorus (► 83).

CAR RENTAL

 Car hire is expensive, partly because of the high accident rate, and is absolutely not recommended in Istanbul. Driving can be a suicidal mission, and traffic is horrendous. Main car-rental agencies are represented at the airport.

TAXIS

 The easiest way to get around is by taxi – yellow and plentiful. Insist on switching on the meter. Avoid cabs at tourist sites offering an expensive fixed rate. Have a map at hand, or the place where you are going written in Turkish.

DRIVING

 Speed limit on motorways: **120kph**

 Speed limit outside urban centres: **90kph**

 Speed limit in urban centres: **50kph**

 Compulsory only in the front, so ask if you want rear seat belts in a hire car.

 Driving outside the city at night can be dangerous as oncoming vehicles often only switch on their lights at the last minute. By then they are so near that their lights may dazzle you. Make sure your lights are as strong as possible.

 Fuel is available in super (four-star equivalent), normal (two-star) and diesel. Unleaded petrol is found at most petrol stations in Istanbul. Larger petrol stations, especially on highways, usually have a shop and a restaurant open 24 hours. Petrol is cheaper than in most European countries and credit cards are generally accepted.

 If you break down call the Turkish Touring and Automobile Association (☎ 282 81 40). Repair garages are numerous and spare parts are readily available, even for foreign cars.

PERSONAL SAFETY

Petty crime is fairly rare in Istanbul, but watch your belongings in busy tourist areas. Avoid wearing a lot of valuable jewellery and only carry your passport if necessary. The police force is omni-present in town, so it is pretty safe to go out at night. Women on their own should stick to the main streets and avoid certain areas around Galata and İstiklâl Caddesi, as well as Beyazıt, where prostitution is rife. Remember the movie *Midnight Express* and avoid buying or using narcotics, as many dealers are connected to the police.

Police assistance:
☎ **155**
from any call box

TELEPHONES

Telephone boxes do not take coins. For local calls buy phone cards or jetons from a post office or special booths. The jetons come as *kücük* (small), *orta* (medium) or *büyük* (large). To make international calls use a post office (PTT) that either has phonecards on sale or a metered phone. To phone Istanbul from abroad dial the international access code followed by 90 (code for Turkey) then 212 for the European side or 216 for the Asian side. The international operator is on 115.

International Dialling Codes	
From Istanbul to:	
UK	00-44
Germany	00-49
USA/Canada	00-1
Netherlands	00-31

POST

Main post office: Yeni Postahane Caddesi, near Sirkeci station. Large branches: İstiklâl Caddesi, in Kadiköy, Üsküdar and Galatasaray. Most open Mon–Sat 8–5, Sun 9–7; international phone offices 24 hours. For poste restante write: name followed by Büyük PTT, Yeni Postahane Caddesi, Sirkeci, Istanbul.

ELECTRICITY

The power supply in Istanbul is 220 volts AC.
Type of socket: round two-pronged sockets with round pins. British visitors will need an adaptor, US visitors a voltage transformer.

TIPS/GRATUITIES

Yes ✓ No ✗		
Restaurants (if service included)	✓	change
Restaurants (service not inc.)	✓	10–15%
Cafés/bars	✓	change
Tour guides	✓	L2–3
Taxis	✓	change
Chambermaids	✓	L2–3
Porters	✓	L1–1.50
Theatre/cinema usherettes	✓	change
Toilets with attendant	✓	change

HEALTH

Insurance
EU health care is not available so a travel insurance policy covering both the European and Asian side is essential.

Dental Services
EU health care is not available so private medical insurance is essential. A few dentists speak English or French. Catherine Feyzioğlu (☎ 233 06 27), Reha Sezgin (☎ 240 33 32) or the German Hospital Dental Clinic (☎ 293 21 50).

Sun Advice
Summers in Istanbul, especially in July and August, can get oppressively hot and sticky, which is why many Istanbulis go to the islands or beaches. Cover up, use a high-factor suncream and make sure you drink plenty of fluids.

Drugs
Turkish chemists (*eczane*) stock all the most common prescribed and unprescribed drugs and will treat minor illnesses. Every district has an all-night pharmacy (*nöbetçi eczane*).

Safe Water
Tap water is reasonably safe but heavily chlorinated, so it is advisable to drink the readily available bottled mineral water.

CONCESSIONS

Students Holders of an International Student Identity Card (ISIC) or an International Youth Card (IYC) get discounts on transport, museum entrance and cinema/theatre tickets. Students can also make use of a number of hostels, including Yücelt Interyouth Hostel next to the Ayasofya (☎ 513 61 50) or the Kadırga Youth Student Hostel in Kumkapı (☎ 527 0218). A FIYTO student card gives free entrance to most sites and museums.

Senior Citizens Senior citizens have no advantages in showing their cards but receive discounts in some cinemas and theatres if they look clearly over 65.

CLOTHING SIZES

Turkey	UK	Rest of Europe	USA	
46	36	46	36	Suits
48	38	48	38	
50	40	50	40	
52	42	52	42	
54	44	54	44	
56	46	56	46	
41	7	41	8	Shoes
42	7.5	42	8.5	
43	8.5	43	9.5	
44	9.5	44	10.5	
45	10.5	45	11.5	
46	11	46	12	
37	14.5	37	14.5	Shirts
38	15	38	15	
39/40	15.5	39/40	15.5	
41	16	41	16	
42	16.5	42	16.5	
43	17	43	17	
34	8	34	6	Dresses
36	10	36	8	
38	12	38	10	
40	14	40	12	
42	16	42	14	
45	18	44	16	
38	4.5	38	6	Shoes
38	5	38	6.5	
39	5.5	39	7	
39	6	39	7.5	
40	6.5	40	8	
41	7	41	8.5	

LANGUAGE

Turkish is not an easy language to pick up while you are visiting the country, but happily many people in Turkey speak English and/or German or French. However, even the most basic attempt at uttering a few words in Turkish will always be greatly appreciated by Istanbulis. Since Atatürk abolished the Arabic script, Turkish is written in the Latin alphabet, but several letters are pronounced differently.

ay = igh as in night   *c* = j   *ç* = ch   *ğ/y* = silent, lengthening the preceding vowel
i = e as in scene   *j* = zh   *ö* = ur   *ş* = sh   *ü* = ew

hotel	*otel*	bath	*banyo*
pension	*pansiyon*	shower	*duş*
single room	*tek kişilik oda*	toilet	*tuvalet*
double room	*iki kişilik oda*	hot water	*sıcak su*
one night	*bir gecelik*	key	*anahtar*
reservation	*reservasyon*	lift	*asansör*
room service	*oda servisi*	sea view	*deniz manzarası*
towel	*havlu*	reception	*resepsiyon*
bank	*banka*	credit card	*kredi kart*
exchange office	*kambiyo*	exchange rate	*döviz kuru*
post office	*PTT or postane*	commission	*komisyon ücreti*
stamp	*pul*	charge	
cheque	*çek*	cashier	*kasiyer*
traveller's	*seyahat çeki*	change	*bozuk para*
cheque		foreign currency	*doviz*
restaurant	*okanta/restoran*	fruit	*meyva*
bill	*hesap*	bread	*ekmek*
breakfast	*kahvaltı*	beer	*bira*
appetisers/	*meze/*	wine	*şarap*
vegetable in	*zeytinyağlılar*	ice	*buz*
olive oil		water	*su*
dessert	*tatlı*	mineral water	*maden suyu*
yoghurt drink	*ayran*	coffee	*kahve*
tea	*çay*	milk	*süt*
aeroplane	*uçak*	return	*gidiş-dönüş*
airport	*havaalanı*	port	*liman*
train station	*istasyon*	car	*araba*
bus	*otobüs*	taxi	*taksi*
bus station	*otogar*	how do I get to...?	*...'a/e nasil*
boat	*vapur/feribot*		*giderim?*
ferry landing	*iskele*	how far is..?	*...ne kadar uzak?*
a ticket to...	*...'a bir bilet*	where is...?	*...nerede?*
yes	*evet*	goodbye	*güle güle* (said by
no	*hayır, yok*		the one staying)
please	*lütfen*	good morning	*günaydin*
thank you	*teşekkür ederim,*	good afternoon	*iyi günler*
	mersi, sağol	goodnight	*iyi geceler*
hello	*merhaba*	excuse me	*pardon*
goodbye	*allahaısmarladık*	how much?	*ne kadar/kaça?*
	(said by the one	open/closed	*açık/kapalı*
	leaving)		

INDEX

Acknowledgements

The Automobile Assocation wishes to thank the following photographers, libraries and
associations for their assistance in the preparation of this book:

J ALLAN-CASH PHOTOLIBRARY 66/7; M BERKMEN 54b, 55b; MARY EVANS PICTURE
LIBRARY 10b, 11b, 14a, 14b; NATURE PHOTOGRAPHERS LTD 13b (P R Sterry), 13C
(R Tidman); PICTURES COLOUR LIBRARY LTD 19b, 62/3, 75b; SADBERK HANIM MUSEUM
66b; SPECTRUM COLOUR LIBRARY F/cover d (Grape juice seller), 41b, 84, 88b;

All remaining pictures are held in the Association's own library (AA PHOTO LIBRARY) and were
taken by C SAWYER with the exception of the following pages: P KENWARD 15a, 15b, 16a, 17a,
17b, 18a, 19a, 20a, 21a, 22a, 23a, 24a, 25a, 26a, 43b, 53, 73b, 90b, 117b, 123c; D MITIDERI
F/Cover a (taxi), 30, 80, 81a, 82, 83a, 85a, 86, 87a, 88a, 89a, 90a; J F PIN 87b, 89b, 123a, 123b;
T SOUTER F/Cover c (carpet), 5b, 6b, 8b, 12b, 16b, 18b, 24b, 32b, 33, 42b, 46b, 50c, 51, 52b, 58,
60b, 60d, 61b, 61c, 63b, 68b, 81b, 85b, 91a, 92/116;

Authors' Acknowledgements

The authors would like to thank the following for their help: Mark Barry and Turkish Airlines,
Peter Espley and the efficient Turkish Tourist Office in London and Mr Gülersoy from the Turkish
Automobile Association, Istanbul.

Copy editor: Sue Gordon   Page layout: Mike Preedy

Dear Essential Traveller

Your comments, opinions and recommendations are very important to us. So please help us to improve our travel guides by taking a few minutes to complete this simple questionnaire.

You do not need a stamp (unless posted outside the UK). If you do not want to cut this page from your guide, then photocopy it or write your answers on a plain sheet of paper.

Send to: **The Editor, AA World Travel Guides, FREEPOST SCE 4598, Basingstoke RG21 4GY.**

Your recommendations...

We always encourage readers' recommendations for restaurants, nightlife or shopping – if your recommendation is used in the next edition of the guide, we will send you a *FREE* AA *Essential* Guide of your choice. Please state below the establishment name, location and your reasons for recommending it.

_____

_____

_____

_____

Please send me **AA *Essential*** _____

(*see list of titles inside the front cover*)

About this guide...

Which title did you buy?

AA *Essential* _____

Where did you buy it? _____

When? m m / y y

Why did you choose an AA *Essential* Guide? _____

_____

_____

_____

_____

Did this guide meet your expectations?

Exceeded ☐   Met all ☐   Met most ☐   Fell below ☐

Please give your reasons _____

_____

_____

_____

continued on next page...

Were there any aspects of this guide that you particularly liked? _____

_____

_____

_____

Is there anything we could have done better? _____

_____

_____

_____

_____

About you...

Name (*Mr/Mrs/Ms*) _____

Address _____

_____

_____ Postcode _____

Daytime tel nos _____

Which age group are you in?
Under 25 ☐ 25–34 ☐ 35–44 ☐ 45–54 ☐ 55–64 ☐ 65+ ☐

How many trips do you make a year?
Less than one ☐ One ☐ Two ☐ Three or more ☐

Are you an AA member? Yes ☐ No ☐

About your trip...

When did you book? m m / y y   When did you travel? m m / y y
How long did you stay? _____
Was it for business or leisure? _____
Did you buy any other travel guides for your trip?
If yes, which ones? _____

_____

Thank you for taking the time to complete this questionnaire. Please send
it to us as soon as possible, and remember, you do not need a stamp
(*unless posted outside the UK*).

Happy Holidays!